18.00

DATE DUE

MAR 0 6 2000			

Demco, Inc. 38-293

D1505922

3 1215 00095 5655

THE ENCYCLOPEDIA OF COOKING TECHNIQUES

THE ENCYCLOPEDIA OF COOKING TECHNIQUES

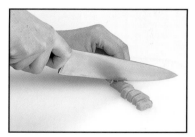

ELIZABETH WOLF COHEN

CHARTWELL
BOOKS, INC.

A QUARTO BOOK

Published by Chartwell Books
A Division of Book Sales, Inc.
114 Northfield Avenue
Edison, New Jersey 08837

This edition produced for sale in the U.S.A., its territories
and dependencies only.

ISBN 0-7858-0613-X

This book was designed and produced by
Quarto Publishing plc
6 Blundell Street
London N7 9BH

Senior Editor Kate Kirby
Senior Art Editor Elizabeth Healey
Designer Sheila Volpe
Photographer Philip Wilkins
Home Economists Katy Holder, Alison Austin
Assistant Home Economist Catherine-Amy Hill
Prop Buyer Susannah Jayes
Picture Manager Giulia Hetherington
Editorial Director Mark Dartford
Art Directors Moira Clinch, Penny Cobb

Typeset by Central Southern Typesetters, Eastbourne
Manufactured by Regent Publishing Services Ltd, Hong Kong
Printed by Leefung-Asco Printers Ltd, China

Contents

Herbs, Spices, and Flavorings

Herbs, spices, and flavorings all contribute to our enjoyment of food. Although most are used in quantities too small to have much nutritional value, they add tremendous scent, flavor, and color to almost everything we cook. Salt and pepper are highly-concentrated seasonings used in most savory food preparations to develop and bring out the flavor of ingredients. Other flavorings, from vanilla and saffron to spirits and wine, give foods a distinctive character.

Herbs

Herbs are the leaves of plants and shrubs with non-woody stems. They add flavor, color, and an appealing aroma, or perfume, as the French say, to many foods. Herbs are very popular in today's cooking, and a wide variety of fresh herbs are available in many supermarkets.

Leafy herbs can be divided into two groups, fragile herbs and robust herbs. Fragile herbs – parsley, tarragon, basil, chervil, and mint – are tender and bruise easily. They are best coarsely chopped and eaten raw as a garnish or very lightly cooked. For longer cooking the stems are used to provide flavor, then removed before the dish is served.

The more robust herbs – thyme, bay, rosemary, sage, savory, oregano, and marjoram – have thicker, sturdier leaves, which are generally strong in flavor and aroma. Because of their strength, these herbs are usually cooked for a longer time and used in stocks and stews.

Some herbal plants, such as dill, celery, angelica, lovage, fenugreek, and cilantro, produce leafy herbs as well as seeds which are treated as spices. In general, the leaves are tender and fragile, and used as tender herbs. The seeds are usually crushed and cooked for a longer time.

BUYING AND STORING HERBS

When buying fresh herbs, choose the healthiest, freshest-looking sprigs with a strong aroma. Avoid musty-smelling herbs with brown-yellow leaves. Buy dried herbs in small containers which can be used within a year. Store them in a cool, dry, dark place.

LARGE BUNCHES OF HERBS ON LONGER STEMS
Cut the stem ends, stand the stalks in a pitcher or bottle of water, and enclose the leaves in a large plastic bag, tying it around the pitcher. Refrigerate, if possible, for several days.

FRESH HERBS WITH SHORT STALKS
Wrap the stalks in a damp paper towel. Keep in a loosely tied plastic bag in the salad drawer of the refrigerator. They will keep for several days.

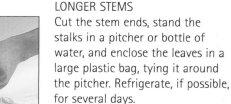

Parsley

Sage

Rosemary

Chervil

Tarragon

Oregano

Lemon thyme

Thyme

Lemon balm

Sorrel

Chives

Mint

Sweet marjoram

Dill

Basil

DRYING AND FREEZING YOUR OWN HERBS

Avoid washing the leaves of fresh herbs unless necessary. Just shake them and wipe off any sand or earth with a soft paper towel or your fingers. Tailor-made stackable drying trays with mesh screens are available from specialty kitchenware stores.

An infusion is made from lemon-scented herbs such as lemon balm, lemon grass, and lemon thyme. Mint, verbena, and dried lime leaves, or rose, camomile, and elderflowers are also popular. Steep *2 tablespoons fresh herbs*, (1 tablespoon dried) in *1 cup/8 oz boiling water* for several minutes. Strain.

TO BUNCH-DRY HERBS
Tie the herbs together with string and hang, stem end up, in a dry warm spot away from direct sunlight. Allow the air to circulate and, if hanging outdoors, bring them in at night when they might hold condensation, which would encourage mold. Alternatively, individual sprigs can be laid flat on baking sheets and dried under the same conditions. Turn them occasionally; when dry, remove the leaves and pack in glass jars. Store as for dried herbs.

MICROWAVE DRYING
To dry herbs in the microwave, put about 6 sprigs of herbs on a double layer of paper towels. Cover with another towel and microwave on full power (100 percent) for 2–3 minutes. Or, small quantities can be dried in the oven. Preheat to the lowest temperature, spread leaves on a rack on a baking sheet lined with cheesecloth and set in the oven. Leave door ajar and stir occasionally until the leaves are crisp and dry.

FREEZING UNCHOPPED HERBS
Tie a small bundle together and dip the heads into boiling water for a few seconds. Plunge into ice water to stop cooking and help set the color. Dry gently, remove the leaves from the stem, and pack into small freezer bags. Use from frozen, adding directly to cooked foods. The most successful results using this method are with parsley and tarragon. Basil, chives, and dill do not need blanching.

FREEZING CHOPPED HERBS
Put a tablespoon of chopped herbs – such as parsley, chives, dill, tarragon, or cilantro – into the bottom of an ice-cube tray compartment. Fill with water, making sure the herbs are covered, and freeze. To use, stir a cube of the ice-herb into stocks, soups, and stews.

CHOPPING FRESH HERBS

It is the aromatic essential oils in the herb which provide flavor and aroma. Strip the leaves from their stems for chopping; reserve the stems for use in stocks and soups.

Pile the leaves on a cutting board and, holding a large chef's knife, rock it back and forth. Continue chopping to the required degree of fineness.

MAKING A BOUQUET GARNI

A *bouquet garni* is one of the most important aromatics in the kitchen. It is used to flavor stocks and many long-cooked stews and braises. A classic bouquet is made with fresh parsley stems, thyme sprigs, and bay leaves, although a stalk of celery or leek is sometimes added. Little bouquet garnis of dried herbs can be bought, but the flavor of a homemade one is superior. Tie the herbs with string, which can be used to remove the bouquet before serving the dish.

The Onion Family

Although technically vegetables, the onion family is used to provide some of our most common flavorings: onion itself, garlic, shallots, leeks, and chives, the only true herb of the family.

Garlic has a somewhat controversial flavor – some people love it; others avoid it at all costs. It is known for its pungency, aroma, and blood-thinning properties, and is used extensively in Mediterranean and Asian cooking. Although it can be roasted as a vegetable, it is most often used in small quantities to enhance other flavors.

There are three kinds of garlic, white – the most commonly seen variety – purple, and red-skinned. They range in flavor from mild to strong, the freshest being the mildest. Elephant garlic, a giant mild variety, is becoming widely available and is ideal for roasting whole as a vegetable.

COOKING WITH GARLIC

Garlic can be used raw in salad dressings, marinades, and dips, or it can be cooked in many dishes. It is frequently added to lightly sweated onions as a base for many other food preparations. After long cooking, the flavor softens and sweetens. Do not allow it to brown when cooking, or it develops a bitter taste.

FRYING GARLIC
If frying garlic with onions, first cook the onions slowly over medium heat in 1–2 tablespoons of butter or oil. Stir in the chopped garlic and cook only 1 minute or until just softened and fragrant. Proceed as recipe directs. *Do not allow to brown.*

AS A FLAVORING
To use as a flavoring only, heat 2 tablespoons (or more) of oil in a skillet over medium-low heat. Add a few garlic cloves and cook slowly, stirring frequently, until soft and lightly colored. Remove the garlic and add the remaining ingredients as directed.

PEELING AND CHOPPING GARLIC

If the garlic is old and has begun to germinate, remove the green center heart, as it has a bitter taste.

SEPARATING CLOVES
To separate the individual cloves, crush the bulb with the palm of your hand or pull off individual cloves with your fingers.

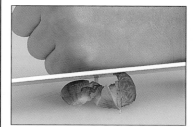

CRUSHING GARLIC
To crush a clove with a knife, set the blade of a large chef's knife on top of the clove and pound with the side of your fist. Remove the skin.

CHOPPING GARLIC
To hand-chop garlic, peel off the papery skin, cut off the top and root end, and chop coarsely or finely with the blade of the knife, as for leafy herbs. Or, chop as for shallots.

BUSY COOKS

Put peeled cloves in a garlic crusher. Squeeze the handles together, pushing the pulp out of the crusher. Use only where a very strong flavor is required.

SHALLOTS

The shallot, a purple-green vegetable, is a variety of onion. Most frequently used in French cooking, it should never be allowed to brown or it will become bitter, like burnt garlic. Finely chopped, it can be used raw in salad dressings or marinades or as a base for fine-flavored sauces.

PREPARING SHALLOTS

1 Using a small, sharp knife, peel the shallot by cutting off the stem and root ends and pull off the brown skin. Sometimes there are 2 sections; separate, if necessary, and set each section, flat-side down, on a cutting board.

2 Slice lengthwise through the shallot just to the root end, but not cutting through it. Pressing down on the curved side with your fingers, slice horizontally in toward the root end, leaving the slices attached.

3 Cut crosswise, allowing the shallot to fall into fine dice.

CHIVES

Chives have a lovely, mild, onion flavor and look pretty as a garnish, whether snipped, chopped, or used whole. Sprinkle over cooked dishes and salads to garnish, or add at the end of cooking.

PREPARING CHIVES

1 Using kitchen scissors, hold a small bunch of chives over a bowl and snip into small pieces.

2 Or, with a knife chop or slice crosswise into tiny pieces.

AS A GARNISH

To use as a garnish for tying small bunches of vegetables, blanch in boiling water for 2–5 seconds and refresh. This makes them supple for tying.

Buying and Using Spices

Nowadays, most spices are widely available in supermarkets and are sold whole or ground. Buy in small quantities as they do lose their potency. Whole spices will keep longer than ground spices. Store in tightly sealed jars in a cool, dry, dark place. Store red spices – such as paprika, cayenne, and hot red chilis – in the refrigerator, where they will keep their strength and color longer.

The cuisines of hot countries such as India, North Africa, Africa, Latin America, and Indonesia use spices most lavishly, perhaps because many spices originate in these countries. Northern and Central Europe use "fragrant" and some "hot" spices such as cinnamon, nutmeg, and cloves, seeds like dill and juniper, and paprika. French and Italian cooking tends to use fresh herbs more than spices, and the Chinese and Japanese use garlic, soy, and ginger more than any other spices.

However, there are several traditional spice mixtures that can be bought or made at home. Curry powder, *garam masala* (a traditional Indian spice mixture), American chili powder, Chinese five-spice powder, French *quatre-espices* (four spices), and the North African *ras-el-hanout* are all better prepared at home with freshly ground spices.

HOT SPICES

Hot spices such as pepper, mustard, chili peppers, ginger, and horseradish add an intense heat and individual flavor to many dishes. These spices need careful preparation and temperate use because they can be overpowering.

COOKING WITH SPICES: MAKING A SPICE BAG

Whole spices are used in pickles, preserves, and other long-cooked dishes, as ground spices can become brittle with long cooking. Some spice berries – such as peppercorns, juniper berries, allspice, mustard seed – should be lightly crushed before cooking, to help them release their flavors. Many recipes advise lightly toasting spices before cooking to release their flavors.

To make a spice bag for pickling or other long-cooked dishes, wrap the whole spices in a square of cotton cheesecloth. Pull the edges together and tie with string, leaving one end long enough to tie to the handle of a cooking utensil. This allows the bag to be found and easily removed at the end of the cooking time.

TOASTING SPICES

To toast whole spices before grinding, put them in a heavy-based skillet and toast over low heat, shaking and stirring gently until they are fragrant. Be careful not to burn them as they scorch easily. Transfer to a plate to cool before grinding.

GRINDING SPICES

Use a mortar and pestle to grind spices, or a small electric coffee grinder; but reserve it for spice-grinding only. To coarsely grind or crack spices, put them in a heavy-duty freezer bag and twist to close. Crush the spices with a heavy skillet or rolling pin.

PEPPER

Pepper berries can be black, white, or green. Black pepper is the dried unripe berry. White pepper is the dried ripened berry, with the outer casing removed. It is less intense than black pepper and often used in cream sauces. Green peppercorns are unripe pepper berries which have a slightly acid taste. They are available preserved in brine or freeze-dried. Green peppercorns preserved in brine should be rinsed and used in

cream sauces for steaks or in other rich meats like duck or venison. If using freeze-dried berries, crush lightly.

Pink peppercorns come from a South American plant related to poison ivy. They have a slightly sharp, acidic flavor, but are primarily used for a decorative effect. Szechuan pepper is a dried berry. Its unique aroma is prized in Chinese cookery. It should be lightly toasted before crushing.

MUSTARD

Mustard can be made from black, white, or brown seeds. Black mustard seeds have the finest flavor, but are difficult to harvest and have largely been replaced by brown seeds, which are more suitable for mechanical production. Yellow seeds, used in most American mustards, are the mildest. Whole seeds appear in pickles, relishes, and chutneys, and in Indian cooking. Ground mustard is mixed with liquid to make prepared mustard. All are used as condiments and in cooking.

Store all mustard in a cool, dry place for up to a year. Refrigerate any opened prepared mustard.

One of the most famous prepared mustard is *Dijon*. It must conform to a certain standard, following a strict recipe of ground black mustard seeds, salt, spices, and wine or wine vinegar.

American mustard is made from yellow mustard seed, salt, vinegar, and spices. The addition of turmeric gives it the bright yellow color associated with ball-park hot dogs.

Most *German mustards* are dark, smooth, and slightly sweet, the result of added caramel.

English mustard is made from a combination of ground dark and light seeds, and is smooth, bright yellow, and very hot. In its powdered form, dry mustard is added to mayonnaise, cheese sauces, and other sauces and dressings.

Chinese mustard is also very hot and sharp. It is sold as a powder for mixing with water or other liquid and used as a condiment or dipping sauce.

Coarse-grain mustards are produced in many countries. The rough texture comes from coarsely ground seeds blended into the mixture.

Dijon

American mustard

German mustard

English mustard

Coarse-grain mustard

COOKING WITH MUSTARD

MAKING PREPARED MUSTARDS
To make prepared mustard from dry mustard powder, blend an equal amount of water, wine, milk, or beer into the measured amount of mustard powder. Allow to stand 10–15 minutes for full flavor to develop.

USING PREPARED MUSTARDS
Add prepared mustards to cream sauces or gravy by whisking just before the end of cooking time. Prolonged cooking inhibits the flavor and intensity of the mustard.

CHILIS

There are dozens of varieties of fresh bell peppers, both hot and sweet. Although sweet peppers are usually treated as vegetables, chili peppers are more often used in small quantities as a spicy flavoring. They range in flavor, color, and degree of hotness. Most of the heat is contained in the seeds and veins. The powerful oils in chili can burn eyes and other sensitive areas, so use rubber gloves when preparing chili peppers and wash all utensils and surfaces well after any contact.

Hot red-pepper flakes and *crushed red pepper* are made from dried, crushed chilis. They are slightly milder than fresh chili.

Cayenne pepper is a very fine chili powder with a very fiery heat. It is used in very small quantities.

Paprika is ground from European varieties of sweet bell peppers. Hungary produces the most flavorful paprikas, ranging from mild and sweet to hot and spicy, used in the famous Hungarian goulash. Also popular in Spain, the seeds and veins are removed before grinding. *Hot red pepper sauce* (Tabasco) is the liquid of salted ground chilis, matured for up to 3 years before bottling. It is used in soups, stews, and Creole and Mexican dishes.

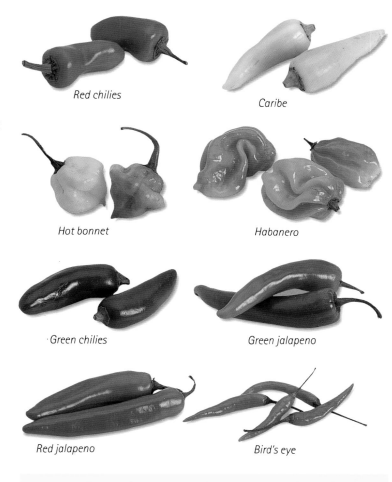

Red chilies

Caribe

Hot bonnet

Habanero

Green chilies

Green jalapeno

Red jalapeno

Bird's eye

BUSY COOKS

Commercial dried chili can be substituted for fresh. If you like, cut off the stalk, shake out the seeds, and put the pepper in a small bowl. Cover with warm water, soak for about 30 minutes, then drain.

PREPARING CHILIS

For a *relatively* mild, yet spicy flavor, core the chilis and remove the seeds before chopping. Wash hands and all equipment thoroughly after use, and wear rubber or plastic gloves.

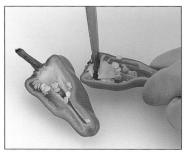

❶ Using a small, sharp knife, cut the chili in half lengthwise. Scrape out the seeds and remove the white veins from the sides.

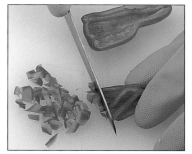

❷ Cut into strips lengthwise, then slice or chop into small dice.

GINGER

Fresh ginger

This underground stem, or rhizome, is available fresh, dried, ground, pickled, candied whole, or crystalized. Its hot yet sweet flavor is essential in Chinese and Indian cooking. Fresh ginger should look plump with a creamy beige color and thin skin. After peeling, it can be grated, chopped, or sliced, and used in sweet and savory dishes. The root can also be dried and grated for use in baking. To keep for up to 3 weeks, wrap in a paper towel in a plastic bag and store in the refrigerator.

Pickled ginger in vinegar is a pink, tangy condiment used to accompany Japanese sushi.

Preserved ginger, either bottled in syrup or crystalized, can be eaten as candy or used in baked goods, custard, ice cream, and fruit salad. Both types can be found in most supermarkets.

Licorice ginger is another variety of preserved ginger. Seasoned with salt and sugar, rhizome licorice is used in Chinese fish dishes. It is found in Chinese supermarkets.

Ground ginger

Pickled ginger

Crystallized ginger

Stem ginger

PREPARING FRESH GINGER

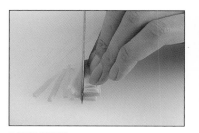

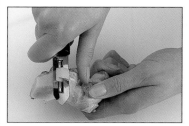

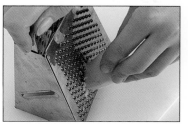

PEELING AND CHOPPING
Using a swivel-bladed vegetable peeler, peel the outside skin exposing the smooth root. Cut lengthwise into thin slices; then cut crosswise and continue chopping into small dice.

JULIENNING
Cut lengthwise into thin slices, then cut lengthwise into thin julienne strips.

GRATING
Rub the peeled ginger against the fine side of a box grater. Use the juice as well as the flesh.

HORSERADISH

Horseradish is a very powerful root related to the cabbage family. Native to Eastern Europe, it is used raw, either grated as a condiment or in other condiments such as seafood sauces.

Prepared horseradish is preserved in vinegar and is the traditional accompaniment to *gefilte fish*, a Jewish festival dish. It is sometimes mixed with beets and called *chrein*. Mixed with whipped or sour cream, it is a classic accompaniment to roast beef, boiled meats, and smoked fish. Heat destroys its flavor, so it is served in cold sauces.

GRATING FRESH HORSERADISH

Horseradish is so strong it is difficult to grate by hand, since the fumes can cause painful tearfulness.

Use the food processor fitted with the grater disk to grate the peeled root. *Do not open the cover.* Allow the grated horseradish to stand 3–5 minutes, then remove the top, holding it away from you; the fumes can be very powerful.

Salt and Salty Flavorings

Salt is an indispensable seasoning for foods, but it must be used carefully. Serious oversalting cannot be remedied, although a little cream, milk, potato, or rice may help to balance the flavor somewhat. Most foods or sauces should be salted at the beginning of cooking, so flavors blend into other ingredients. Stocks and sauces that are reduced to concentrate flavor should not be salted until the end of cooking, if at all. Salty ingredients such as bacon and cheese may negate the need for salt. Used in bread and pastry-making both to bring out flavor and to inhibit the yeast, salt also attracts moisture, so it is used to degorge eggplants and cucumbers. For the same reason, meat should be seasoned just before cooking, since the salt draws out the juices.

Salty flavorings include soy sauce and meat and yeast extracts.

SALT GLOSSARY

Table salt Soft, fine, sea or mined salt, the most commonly used condiment which dissolves instantly. Most table salt has iodine added.

Kosher salt Large, irregular crystals, free from additives and iodine, with a "less salty" taste – for sprinkling large areas or salting large quantities of water.

Sea or bay salt Refined from evaporated salts of shallow salt water pans, considered superior to table salt. The grayish French *gros sel* is considered the best.

Rock salt Roughly crushed chunks of mined salt, used in ice cream makers and for displaying seafood.

Flavored salts Salts flavored with celery, onion, garlic, or sesame;

used to season certain foods.

Sour salt Not a true salt, but crystalized citric acid of citric salt, lemon, or lime, used in Middle Eastern cooking.

Light salts/salt substitutes For use in salt-restricted diets, these contain potassium and/or sodium chloride.

Table salt   Sea salt   Bay salt   Rock salt

Celery salt   Garlic salt   Onion salt

SOY SAUCE

Soy sauce is made from naturally fermented soybeans and wheat which have been salted, then aged to mature and develop flavor.

Light soy sauce is paler in color, but saltier than dark soy sauce. It is best for cooking.

Dark soy sauce is aged longer, giving it a richer hue and thicker consistency. It is used in more robust dishes and as a dipping sauce.

Japanese soy sauce, called *shoyu,* is generally considered superior, as it is always naturally fermented.

Light soy

Dark soy

FISH SAUCES

Many Asian cuisines use a fermented fish sauce to give a salty flavor to food. The Thai *nam pla* and Vietnamese *nuoc nam* are the most widely available. They are used in savory dishes and as dips for fried foods.

Oyster sauce is a Chinese fish sauce made from oysters and wheat, corn, or rice.

Anchovy paste, made from mashed, salted anchovies, gives a salty but surprisingly "non-fishy" flavor to many meat, vegetable, and fish dishes.

MEAT AND YEAST EXTRACTS

Popular in Britain and Australia, meat and yeast extracts are used to reinforce the flavor of soups, stocks, sauces, and meat dishes. Meat extracts are made from a process of extracting flavor from beef; yeast extracts are made from salt and brewer's yeast, a by-product of beer making.

Olives and Capers, Essences and Extracts

In addition to being excellent finger food, olives contribute a pungent flavor to many salads, pizzas, pasta sauces, and meat and duck dishes. They are also the source of nature's most delicious oils. Olives can be black (ripe) or green (unripe), large or small, brine-cured, dry-salt-cured, or a combination. Capers have a sharp, salty flavor which enhances many dishes.

ESSENCES AND EXTRACTS

Essences and extracts used to flavor food come from aromatic plant oils. Nowadays, many are produced synthetically. These flavorings are highly volatile and dissipate quickly in air or when exposed to heat, so they should be added to cold or cooling foods. When used in cakes and cookies, cream them into the butter or fat, which slows their vaporization. In general, 1 teaspoon extract is used to flavor 2 cups/1 pint liquid or 1 pound dry ingredients, but this depends on the recipe and personal taste. Vanilla and almond are probably the most commonly-used extracts, although lemon, mint, spearmint, cinnamon, and clove are also popular. Flower-based extracts such as rosewater and orangeflower water are used in Middle-Eastern, Indian, and Mediterranean cooking. They have a powerful perfume. Flower waters and all essences and extracts should be stored in a cool, dark place, and preferably in dark bottles.

OLIVES AND CAPERS

PITTING OLIVES
Use a cherry pitter to remove the pits before chopping, slicing, or adding whole to various dishes.

USING CAPERS
Capers are the pickled buds of the Mediterranean caperberry plant. They are always cured in salt or vinegar. Care is needed since heat brings out the saltiness.

Rinse and drain capers before adding to the dishes at the end their cooking time.

VANILLA

Vanilla is probably the most frequently used flavor in baking. The so-called vanilla bean is the pod of a tropical orchid. Picked unripe and sun-cured for up to a year to release its rich flavor, these long, black beans are essential for flavoring ice creams, custards, sauces, and syrups. If used to infuse a syrup or custard, the pod can be rinsed, drained, dried, and used again.

PREPARING VANILLA
❶ Using a small, sharp knife, split the vanilla bean lengthwise. Use to infuse hot liquid such as milk or a sugar syrup 20–30 minutes.

❷ For a stronger flavor, split the pod and, using the tip of the knife, scrape out the seeds. Add to liquids for ice creams, puddings and custards.

VANILLA SUGAR
Push a split vanilla bean into a 1-pound jar of sugar and leave, covered, for 2–3 days or longer. Use to flavor any recipe where a hint of vanilla is called for.

Flavoring with Wines and Spirits

WINE
Wine can add great substance to many dishes, but unless it is reduced during cooking, it can impart a harsh, raw, or acidic taste. Some of the alcohol must be cooked out during long cooking, as in stews and braised dishes, or the wine can be reduced on top of the stove to concentrate its flavor in sauces. The characteristics of the wine will be intensified in cooking, so follow the rule that if a wine is good enough to drink, you can cook with it. Use robust red wines for red meat and game, roasts, rich brown sauce, and gravy, and lighter red or white wines for veal, chicken, and fish. Avoid using wine with salty or smoked foods and those with strong citrus flavors.

SPIRITS, BRANDIES, AND LIQUEURS
Spirits and brandies are used at the start of cooking to add flavor and body to a dish, or just before serving to accentuate a robust flavor. They are often used in meat pâtés and terrines as well as fruitcakes and they act as a preservative. Fortified wines such as sherry, port, Madeira, and Marsala are often added to sauces at the end of cooking or to deglaze pans. Liqueurs and cordials are used in desserts. If used with a stronger spirit, they can be flambéed.

FLAMBE
Dishes flambéed with spirits and alcohols are part of the classic repertoire. Once heated, the alcohol ignites and boils off. While making a dramatic effect, the flaming helps to burn off raw flavors, helps to caramelize other sugars in sauces, and concentrates the flavor.

❶ Heat the spirit, brandy, or liqueur in a small saucepan or ladle over medium-high heat until bubbles form around the edge; do not boil.

❷ Light the liquid with a long taper or extra-long match.

REDUCING WINE

❶ To reduce and concentrate wine, add it as all or part of the cooking liquid to meat or game dishes. The long, slow cooking will evaporate the alcohol naturally, leaving a concentrated wine flavor.

❷ To reduce wine for use in sauces or for deglazing, pour into a saucepan and allow it to reduce by half at a simmer over medium-high heat.

DEGLAZING A PAN

To deglaze a pan, remove any cooked meats, then pour off excess fat. Add the wine or spirits, scraping up all the bits on the bottom of the pan.

❸ Pour over the heated food (crêpes, plum pudding, or steaks, etc.) and spoon over, basting the food, until the flames die out, which will happen as soon as the alcohol is evaporated.

❹ Use a skewer to poke holes in a fruitcake and pour in small amounts of brandy. Keep the fruitcake wrapped in a cheesecloth or foil and continue "soaking" as desired.

Vinegar

Vinegar, from the French *vin aigre* or "sour wine," can be a versatile flavoring. Vinegar is created when a naturally fermented alcohol such as wine, sherry, or cider is converted to acetic acid by adding a bacteria. Nowadays this is done under controlled conditions to produce vinegar.

Commonly used in salad dressings, pickles, preserves, and chutneys, it is also important for adding zest to sauces and as a tenderizer in marinades. Flavored vinegars are ideal for deglazing cooking juices of rich meats such as liver and duck. Store vinegars in a cool dark place, since their flavor dissipates with age. Vinegars vary in strength (degrees of acidity) and flavor. Roughly speaking, the degree of acetic acid in vinegar will be the same as the degree of wine which produces it, most wine vinegars will be about 5–6 percent.

MAKING HERB VINEGARS

Use a good quality white or red wine vinegar, or cider vinegar. Lightly bruise the herbs first to allow them to give off their flavors.

1 Put about 2 oz fresh, lightly bruised herbs in a sterilized heatproof bottle or jar. Heat about 2 cups/1 pint vinegar until bubbles begin to form around the edge and pour over the herbs.

2 Seal and store in a cool, dark place for at least 2 weeks. Turn the bottle occasionally.

3 If you like, add a sprig of the same fresh herb to a pretty bottle, for an attractive presentation and identification. Strain the flavored vinegar through a paper coffee filter or a cheesecloth-lined strainer in the bottle. Seal the bottle tightly, label, and store in a cool, dark place for up to a year.

VINEGAR GLOSSARY

Wine vinegar Red or white, most wine vinegars have about 6 percent acetic acid and a pleasant wine aroma and pungency without being too harsh. Use in salad dressings, marinades, pickles, and sauces.

Sherry vinegar A highly prized vinegar made from Spanish sherry, with a fragrant, nutty flavor. Use in salad dressings, sprinkled over vegetables, or to deglaze sautéed calf or chicken liver.

Raspberry and other fruit vinegars Made by marinating raspberries or other fruit in wine vinegar, before straining. Fruit-flavor vinegars add character to salad dressings, chicken, duck, and liver dishes, and even to fruit salads.

Cider vinegar A milder vinegar made from apple ciders, it is especially good in dressing for coleslaws and other vegetables, as well as in pickles and milder chutneys.

White (distilled) vinegar A harsh vinegar made from grain alcohol. Widely used for pickles and chutney.

Rice vinegar Made from rice, this vinegar has a pale to clear color with a mild, sweetish flavor. Used in Chinese and Japanese cooking, it is excellent in salad dressings, dipping sauces, noodle dishes, and pickles.

Balsamic vinegar Extremely popular, this highly prized vinegar is made from white grape juice aged for years in wooden casks. It becomes dark brown and almost syrupy, with a sweet-and-sour flavor. It is excellent for sprinkling on broiled vegetables or salads and even strawberries. The finest aged vinegars from Modena, Italy, can be ten years old and as expensive as fine wines.

Wine vinegar *Sherry vinegar* *Raspberry vinegar* *Cider vinegar* *Rice vinegar* *Balsamic vinegar*

Stocks and Sauces

Stocks and sauces are the foundation of much good cooking. *Stock*, a thin flavorful liquid, forms the base of many great soups, sauces, stews, and braises. In fact, the French word for stock is "fond," which means base or foundation. *Sauces* are thickened liquids used to add flavor, moisture, richness, and visual appeal to many dishes, both sweet and savory.

Types of Stock

There are four basic kinds of stock which, although they use similar combinations of the same ingredients, have different characteristics.

White stocks are not really white but pale. They are generally made by simmering beef, veal, or chicken bones in water with vegetables and seasonings. The stock is pale in color with a mild but rich flavor. Peel the onions if you require a very pale stock.

Brown stock is made from beef, veal, chicken, or game bones in water with vegetables and seasonings. These are browned and caramelized first before being simmered. The stock has a rich, dark color and full flavor.

Fish stock or fumet is slightly different in that it cooks for a relatively short period of time, about 25 minutes. The bones are not browned, and wine or lemon juice is usually added, resulting in a pale but strongly flavored stock. *Shellfish stock* can be made like fish stock, or the carcasses of the crustaceans can be browned in oil before simmering; it depends on its intended use.

Court bouillon is a pale, vegetable-based stock, which contains wine. It is usually cooled before being used to poach fish or delicate meats like sweetbreads.

STOCK INGREDIENTS

The basic stock ingredients are bones, vegetables, aromatics, seasoning, and water. Bones are the most important ingredient, providing flavor, richness, and color. It is becoming more and more difficult to find beef and veal bones, so buy them when they are available and keep them in the freezer until you have enough to make a large pot of stock. Beef- and veal-based stocks need 6–8 hours; chicken stock will take about 5–6 hours.

The best bones for fish stock are from lean white fish like sole, flounder, turbot, and whiting. Do not use oily or strong-flavored fish like salmon, swordfish, tuna, or mackerel. Avoid large pieces of skin as they can impart bitterness to the stock. Make stocks from turkey, lamb, and ham bones only for recipes using these ingredients.

Onions, carrots, celery, leeks, mushrooms, and tomatoes are the most commonly used stock vegetables. It is unnecessary to peel them; in fact, onion skins are often added to give brown stock extra color. Vegetables like cabbage, broccoli, peppers, turnips, and others with easily detectable flavors are not suitable. For long-cooking beef stock, cut the vegetables into 2–3-inch pieces; for short-cooking fish stock, simply dice them coarsely. Most stocks include aromatics tied together in a *bouquet garni* (page 8).

WHITE STOCK: WHITE VEAL STOCK

Use veal, beef, or chicken bones or a combination of all of them, cut into pieces. Always try to use at least one veal bone. Bones for white stock can be blanched, if you like. Cover with cold water, and bring to a boil, skimming off the foam as it rises to the surface. Drain and rinse, then start the stock.

INGREDIENTS
4–5 lb veal bones, cracked or
    cut in pieces
2 large onions, trimmed but
    unpeeled and quartered
3 carrots, cut in 3–4-inch pieces
1–2 stalks celery, cut into pieces
2 leeks, washed and cut in
    3–4-inch pieces
1–2 cloves garlic, crushed
large bouquet garni (p.8)
1 tablespoon black peppercorns

❶ Blanch the veal bones, if desired, following the directions above. Put the bones and all remaining ingredients into a large stockpot. Add enough cold water to cover all ingredients by at least 1 inch.

❷ Set the stockpot over medium-high heat and bring to a boil. As liquid comes to a boil, skim off any foam which rises to the surface. Reduce heat to very low and simmer for about 6 hours, skimming occasionally. The liquid should barely simmer.

WHITE STOCK: WHITE VEAL STOCK CONTINUED

3 Ladle stock through a cheesecloth-lined strainer or colander into a large bowl. Cool as quickly as possible.

4 When stock is chilled, use a flat spoon to scrape and lift the solidified fat off the surface. Store stock in the refrigerator for up to 5 days or freeze up to a year. Bring to a boil before using in other recipes.

5 For easier storage, reduce the stock to half its volume by boiling over high heat. Cool, then chill. Freeze in small quantities in plastic freezer bags or ice-cube trays. To use, dilute with as much water as required.

STOCK VARIATIONS

Chicken stock Substitute about 3 pounds of chicken necks and backs for half the veal bones and proceed as for White Veal Stock. Simmer for 4–5 hours.

Brown beef stock Substitute 3 pounds of beef bones for half the veal bones, or replace all veal bones with beef bones.

Brown chicken stock Substitute 3 pounds of chicken necks and backs for half the veal bones and proceed as for White Veal Stock.

Vegetable stock A good vegetable stock can be made using a wide variety of vegetables in even proportions, so that the flavor of no one vegetable overpowers another. Brown them, if you like, before adding water; this gives the stock a richer flavor. Add a little tomato paste for color. An hour or two will generally be enough cooking time to extract maximum flavor.

BROWN STOCK: BROWN VEAL/BEEF STOCK

Use the same ingredients as for White Stock, adding 2 halved tomatoes, and proceed as follows. Cut a third onion in half and singe; see Step 1.

Preheat oven to 450°F. Put the bones in a large roasting pan and roast until well browned, about 45 minutes, turning occasionally.

1 Add the cut-up vegetables, except for the tomatoes, and roast 20 minutes longer, until well browned. For extra color, hold half an onion over an electric plate or gas burner until completely singed.

2 Transfer browned bones and vegetables to a large stockpot. Add the onion and remaining tomatoes, the bouquet garni, and the seasonings. Set the roasting pan over direct heat. Skim off any fat, add 2 cups/1 pint water, bring to a boil, stirring to deglaze the pan.

3 Pour into the stockpot, and add enough cold water to cover the bones. Bring to a boil, skimming off any foam which rises to the surface. Proceed as for White Veal Stock.

GLAZES

Glazes are highly reduced and concentrated stocks, used in soups and sauces to intensify flavors. One gallon of stock is necessary to produce 1–2 cups/8–16 oz of glaze. Meat glaze is made from reduced brown stock; fish glaze from reduced fish stock. Glazes keep in the refrigerator for weeks.

FISH STOCK

Be sure to wash the fish bones well before using for stock. Do *not* blanch them, as blanching removes too much flavor. Sweat fish bones lightly beforehand in a little oil or butter to bring out even more flavor. If a completely fat-free stock is required, put all the ingredients, except the oil or butter, into the stockpot. Cover with enough cold water and begin at Step 3.

❶ Heat about 1 tablespoon oil or butter in a large stockpot over medium heat. Add a finely chopped onion (or 3–4 finely chopped shallots). Cook 3–4 minutes until softened but not colored. Add a chopped leek, carrot, celery stalk, and 4 oz chopped mushrooms. Cook 3–4 more minutes.

❷ Add about 1½ lb cut-up fish bones and stir well. Cook 2–3 minutes, then add 1 cup/8 oz dry white wine or juice of ½ lemon, and enough cold water to cover. Drop in a bouquet garni and a teaspoon of lightly crushed peppercorns.

❸ Bring to a boil and skim off any foam which rises to the surface. Reduce heat to low and simmer gently for 20–25 minutes. Strain as for veal stock. Cool, then refrigerate.

Sauces

Sauces are seasoned, thickened liquids which should have good texture, firm body, and full flavor, but should not overpower the food they accompany. There are many kinds, but most fall into two categories; *thickened* and *emulsified* sauces. Others vary from a simple melted or clarified butter to sophisticated purées and reductions.

THICKENED SAUCES

A *roux*, a cooked paste of equal amounts of fat and flour, is the most commonly-used thickener for white sauces (*béchamel* and *veloutés*) and brown sauces. Cook a roux over medium heat before adding liquid, to eliminate any raw, floury taste and to help prevent lumps from forming. A white roux should be cooked for about 1 minute, a blond or straw-colored roux, for 2–3 minutes, and a brown roux – often used in Creole or Cajun cooking – for 5 minutes or longer to color sufficiently.

EMULSIFIED SAUCES

Emulsified sauces include ingredients – most often, egg or egg yolks and a fat such as butter or oil – which normally do not form a stable suspension or mixture. By vigorous beating or shaking, the ingredients can be *emulsified* to form a smooth sauce in stable suspension. The most important emulsified sauces are *Hollandaise*, a warm sauce, and *mayonnaise*, a cold emulsified sauce. *Béarnaise* is made the same way as Hollandaise, but is flavored with a reduction of vinegar, shallots, and tarragon which gives it its characteristic sweet/tangy flavor. White butter sauces, popular with chefs since nouvelle cuisine, are made without egg yolks and so have more of a tendency to separate. The quality of all these sauces depends on using the best eggs and butter or oil. Emulsified sauces are famous for being difficult because they separate or curdle so easily.

DIFFERENT METHODS FOR THICKENING SAUCES

Some sauces are best thickened at the last minute. Last-minute thickeners include cornstarch, arrowroot, and kneaded butter (*beurre manié*). An egg and cream liaison can also be used to thicken and enrich a sauce at the last minute.

TO MAKE A ROUX
Melt butter or oil in a heavy-based saucepan over medium heat. Add the flour all at once and stir to make a smooth paste which bubbles and foams. Cook the roux or paste for 1–5 minutes, depending on the color desired, stirring constantly.

TO THICKEN A SAUCE WITH CORNSTARCH, ARROWROOT, OR POTATO STARCH

Dissolve 2–3 teaspoons starch with 2–3 teaspoons cold water or stock, stirring to form a paste. Gradually stir into the boiling liquid. It will thicken almost immediately. Chinese stir-fries and fruit sauces are often thickened this way.

TO THICKEN WITH KNEADED BUTTER

Use a fork to cream together equal quantities of softened butter and flour. Whisk small pieces of kneaded butter into the boiling sauce, continuing to add small pieces of the kneaded butter until the sauce is thickened to the desired consistency. One ounce kneaded butter will thicken about 1 cup/8 oz liquid. It will also enrich the taste and texture.

TO THICKEN WITH AN EGG AND CREAM LIAISON

Beat 1 egg yolk into 2 tablespoons heavy cream. Bring 2 cups/ 1 pint thin sauce or liquid to a boil. Stir a little of the hot sauce into the egg mixture.

Then remove the sauce from the heat and whisk the egg mixture into the sauce. Return the pan to the heat, whisking constantly until the sauce thickens. Do not boil unless the

sauce contains flour to stabilize it. Serve immediately, as this sauce is difficult to reheat.

Because of their neutral base, white sauces are extremely versatile. They are used to bind soufflés, croquettes, soups, egg dishes, and gratins, and to coat many foods. The texture should be smooth and rich, and have the consistency of heavy cream. The taste should be milky, with no hint of raw flour. A plain white sauce is made with butter, flour, and milk only. A béchamel sauce adds a clove-studded onion to infuse the milk before making the sauce, or a small amount of finely chopped onion, which is sweated in the butter or oil before adding the flour. Béchamel is thus the more flavorsome.

For Thin White Sauce or Béchamel (to thicken soups or sauces) Use ½ oz *butter* and ½ oz *flour* to thicken 1 cup/8 oz *milk*.

For Thick White Sauce or Béchamel (to bind soufflés, etc.) Use 1 oz *butter* and 1 oz *flour* to thicken 1 cup/½ pint *milk*.

INGREDIENTS
1 cup/8 oz milk
1 onion, cut into halves and studded with 4 whole cloves (optional)
1 bay leaf (optional)
1½ tablespoons butter
1½ tablespoons all-purpose flour
pinch of grated nutmeg
salt and white pepper

❶ (For plain white sauce, omit this step completely.) Put the milk in a saucepan with the clove-studded onion halves, peppercorns, and bay leaf. Bring to a boil over medium heat, stirring occasionally to prevent sticking. Remove from the heat. Leave to infuse, covered for 15 minutes.

❷ Melt the butter in a medium saucepan over medium-high heat. Add the flour and whisk constantly until blended and foaming, about 1 minute.

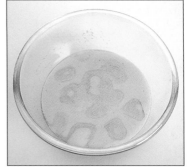

❸ Gradually strain the milk into the roux and bring back to a boil. Boil for 1 minute, whisking constantly, until the sauce thickens. Season with the nutmeg, salt, and pepper; simmer for 5–10 minutes. The sauce can be used immediately.

❹ If not using immediately, strain or pour into a bowl. Dot the surface with flakes of butter; as the butter melts over the surface it prevents a skin from forming. Alternatively, press plastic wrap directly against the surface to prevent a skin from forming.

VELOUTE

A Velouté is often made from the liquid used in cooking the main ingredient, such as that used in poaching fish and chicken, or for veal, as in a *blanquette*. Additional liquid is added to the roux at the beginning to make a very thin sauce. Simmering for 15 minutes to 1 hour thickens the sauce and intensifies the flavor. The long, slow cooking gives it a velvety consistency – hence the name velouté, or "velvety." Stir the sauce frequently to prevent scorching and skim from time to time.

INGREDIENTS
1½ cups/12 oz white veal, chicken, or fish stock
1½ tablespoons butter
1½ tablespoons all-purpose flour
2–3 tablespoons heavy cream or *crème fraîche* (optional)
½ teaspoon lemon juice
salt and white pepper

❶ In a small saucepan, over high heat, bring the stock to a boil. Meanwhile melt the butter in a heavy-based saucepan over medium heat. Pour in the flour and whisk until blended and foaming. Cook until the roux is a golden straw color, 2–3 minutes, stirring constantly. Remove the pan from the heat and cool slightly.

❷ Whisk in the stock and return the pan to the heat. Bring to a boil, whisking constantly until it thickens. Simmer the sauce at least ½ hour up to an hour, stirring frequently and skimming from time to time. Add the cream, if using. Season with the lemon juice, salt and pepper, and boil again.

BROWN SAUCES

The most famous brown sauce, Espagnole, is made with a rich brown stock and a gently cooked brown roux. Although this rich sauce has robust yet fine flavor, it is time-consuming and requires skill; a brown roux is tricky to make without scorching or separating. The sauce is intensified by adding fine (originally Spanish) ham and tomato paste, which adds to the glossy brown color. Although it can be served by itself, it is also the base of many rich, dark French sauces such as Demiglaze, Sauce Robert, and Sauce Madere.

Nowadays, many cooks use a last-minute thickener like arrowroot or potato starch, which produce a lighter sauce.

❶ To make a basic brown sauce, bring 1½ cups/12 oz rich brown stock to a boil over medium-high heat and reduce to about two-thirds its original volume. In a small cup, dissolve 1–2 teaspoons arrowroot or potato starch in 2 tablespoons Madeira or cold water. (The amount of starch depends on the thickness desired; dissolve the minimum, add half, then add more if required.)

❷ Stir the paste, then stir into the boiling stock; the sauce will thicken immediately. If you like, stir in ½ teaspoon tomato paste to enrich the color. Simmer 2 minutes longer. Season with salt, if necessary, and pepper.

CLARIFYING BUTTER

Clarified butter is a way of separating the milky solids (whey) from the pure butterfat. Once clarified, it can be served as a simple sauce, used for frying, or to help stabilize sauces like Hollandaise and Béarnaise.

❶ Put the butter in a small pan and melt over low heat; do not allow the butter to boil.

❷ Remove from the heat and tilt the pan slightly. Using a flat spoon, skim off any foam from the surface. Pour into a small bowl, leaving the milky solids behind. Cool, if recipe directs.

CLASSIC HOLLANDAISE

INGREDIENTS
3 egg yolks
3 tablespoons water
salt and cayenne or white
    pepper
¾ cup/6 oz clarified unsalted
    butter
1–2 teaspoons lemon juice

❶ In a small, heavy-based saucepan (non-aluminum), whisk the egg yolks, water, salt, and pepper, until well-blended.

❷ Set the saucepan over low heat and begin whisking vigorously and constantly until the mixture is thick and creamy and leaves a visible trail on the bottom of the pan. (Remove the pan from the heat occasionally to avoid overheating and curdling the egg yolks.)

❸ Remove from the heat, and slowly and gradually whisk in the clarified butter, drop by drop. As the sauce thickens and absorbs the butter, begin pouring it in a very thin stream until the butter is incorporated (leaving any milky solids in the pan). Season with lemon juice and more salt and pepper if necessary.

BUSY COOKS

Both Hollandaise and Béarnaise can be made in a blender or food processor, in which case the egg yolks do not need heating; however, the clarified butter needs to be just about boiling.

❶ Put the eggs, water, salt, and pepper into the blender or food processor. Process 10 seconds, until light and foamy.

❷ With the machine running, slowly and gradually pour the bubbling butter through the top of the feed tube, drop by drop, until the sauce thickens and absorbs the butter. Begin pouring it in a very thin stream until it is incorporated (leave any milky solids in the pan). Season as in step 3, left.

BEARNAISE SAUCE

Béarnaise is made in much the same way as Hollandaise, but a pungent reduction is made before adding the egg yolks and butter. The reduction should be reduced to about a tablespoon. Remove the pan from the heat occasionally while whisking (Step 2), to avoid overheating and curdling the egg yolks.

INGREDIENTS
3 tablespoons white wine
    vinegar
3 tablespoons dry white wine
10 peppercorns, lightly crushed
2–3 shallots, finely chopped
2 tablespoons fresh chopped
    tarragon
1 tablespoon water
3 egg yolks
¾ cup/6 oz clarified sweet
    butter
salt and white pepper
cayenne pepper

❶ Put the vinegar, wine, peppercorns, shallots, and 1 tablespoon chopped tarragon in a small, heavy-based saucepan. Bring to a boil over medium-high heat and simmer until reduced to a tablespoon of liquid. Remove from the heat and stir in a tablespoon cold water.

❷ Add the egg yolks and season with salt and pepper, whisking to blend. Return to low heat and whisk vigorously and constantly, until the mixture is very thick and creamy and leaves a visible trail on the bottom of the pan.

❸ Remove from the heat. Slowly and gradually whisk in the clarified butter, drop by drop. As the sauce thickens and absorbs the butter, begin pouring it in a very thin stream, until the butter is incorporated (leaving any milky solids in the pan).

❹ Strain the sauce, pushing it through the strainer with a ladle or wooden spoon and stir in the remaining tarragon and adjust seasoning.

WHITE BUTTER SAUCE: WHITE WINE BUTTER SAUCE

These fashionable, extremely rich and delicious sauces are more unstable than the classic emulsions because no egg yolks are used. The base is usually a reduction of wine, vinegar, stock, or pan juices. To avoid separation, the butter must be very cold when it is beaten in so that it doesn't melt before it can be incorporated. Although this technique can be mastered, it is possible to "cheat." Adding a tablespoon of heavy cream or a teaspoon of cornstarch to the reduction helps hold the emulsion and stabilize the sauce.

INGREDIENTS
3 tablespoons dry white wine
3 tablespoons white wine vinegar
2 shallots, finely chopped
1 tablespoon heavy cream or crème fraîche (optional)
1 cup/8 oz very cold unsalted butter, cut into small dice
salt and white pepper

❶ In a small heavy-based pan (not aluminum) bring the wine, vinegar, and shallots to a boil. Boil until reduced to about 1 tablespoon. If using the cream, stir in and boil again until reduced.

❷ Begin whisking in the butter over medium-high heat, piece by piece, until a smooth creamy sauce begins to form. The French call this "mounting" the sauce with butter.

❸ As the sauce emulsifies, add the butter 2–3 pieces at a time, whisking constantly over high heat until it just begins to boil and all the butter has been incorporated. Season and strain, if you like.

VINAIGRETTE

Vinaigrette is an unstable emulsion of vinegar and oil, Dijon mustard, and seasonings. By whisking or shaking vigorously, the mustard helps to emulsify the oil and vinegar, but it will separate on standing or mixing with salad leaves or vegetables.

Although the classic proportions are 3:1 oil to vinegar, the proportions will vary depending on the strength of the mustard and vinegar, so adjust to your taste. Add herbs, garlic, and a little chopped shallot, if you like.

MAYONNAISE

This delicious sauce is used in salads, sandwiches, and as part of other sauces. It can be varied by using different oils, herbs, and other flavorings.

Mayonnaise can also be made in a blender, food processor, or with an electric mixer. Make sure all the ingredients are at room temperature and, if making by hand, set the bowl on a towel to keep it from sliding around.

INGREDIENTS
2 egg yolks
2 tablespoons lemon juice or white wine vinegar
1–2 tablespoons Dijon mustard (optional)
salt and cayenne or white pepper
1½ cups/12 oz olive or vegetable oil, or half of each

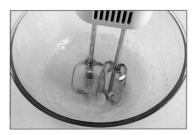

❶ To make mayonnaise, put the egg yolks, half the lemon juice or vinegar, mustard, and salt and pepper into a bowl. Using a wire whisk or electric mixer, beat until creamy and well blended, about 1 minute. Begin adding the oil slowly and gradually, drop by drop, whisking constantly.

❷ As the sauce begins to thicken, begin pouring in the oil in a very slow steady stream until all the oil is incorporated, whisking constantly. Whisk in the remaining lemon juice or vinegar and season, if necessary. (If the sauce separates, slowly whisk it into an egg yolk or a tablespoon of Dijon mustard until it emulsifies.)

❶ Put 2 tablespoons white or red wine vinegar or lemon juice into a small bowl. Whisk in a tablespoon of Dijon mustard and salt and pepper to taste.

❷ Gradually whisk in 6–8 tablespoons of oil of your choice. Olive oil on its own may be too strong, so blend it with a good-quality vegetable oil to your taste.

🥄 Remember, mayonnaise is made with raw egg yolks which can harbor *salmonella* bacteria. Pregnant women, children, and the elderly should avoid undercooked or raw eggs.

Dairy Products and Eggs

Dairy foods and eggs form part of the foundation of Western cuisine. Consumed as foods in their own right, they are also the basis of soups, sauces, puddings, custards, batters, cakes, ice creams, toppings, mousses, and many desserts. They are very nutritious, and are enduringly popular.

Dairy Products

MILK

Most milk and milk products consumed in the U.S. are produced from cows' milk, but goat, sheep, and buffalo milk is appreciated in many parts of the world. Milk is the most basic of all foods and one of the first consumed by humans. Mothers' milk constitutes a complete diet, and cows' milk contains many nutrients, vitamins, and calcium. Not only is it a popular beverage drunk on its own or flavored, it also provides texture, flavor, color, and nutritional value to many cooked or prepared dishes.

Most milk is is *pasteurized* to kill harmful bacteria and improve its keeping qualities. The milk is heated to 161°F and kept at that temperature for 15 seconds. *Ultra-pasteurized* milk is heated to 275°F for 2 to 4 seconds. This process destroys all bacteria and extends shelf life dramatically. UHT (*ultra-high temperature processing*) processes milk at an even higher temperature (280°–300°F) for 2 to 6 seconds, so it can be stored without refrigeration for up to 3 months. Once opened, all processed milk should be treated like fresh milk and refrigerated. (Both milk and cream scorch easily when heated. Prevent this by first rinsing the pan with water. Then heat slowly, stirring occasionally.)

CREAM

Cream is the fatty portion of fresh milk which rises to the surface in a thick layer when milk is left to stand. Modern methods produce cream by centrifugal separator. The high-fat content gives cream a rich, buttery flavor and velvety texture. It is used to enrich soups and sauces, and to give body to puddings, custards, and mousses. Added to baked goods and pastries, it provides extra richness and tenderness. Cream is used as a sauce in itself and is the basis for all ice creams and other frozen desserts.

Whipping cream Because of its high-fat content, cream holds its shape when whipped. Whipped cream can be used as a garnish or added to mousses and parfaits to create other puddings or fillings. Whipped cream can be frozen, then defrosted just before using.

MILK GLOSSARY

Whole milk contains at least 3.5 percent milk fat.

Low fat milk contains from 0.5 to 2 percent milk fat, sometimes labeled "99 percent fat free" or "1 percent low fat." Increasingly popular because of current concerns about diet and cholesterol.

Skim milk (non-fat milk). The fat content must be less than 0.5 percent. Most skim milk is fortified with vitamins A and D.

Acidophilus milk is a cultured milk made from skim or low-fat milk. This helps maintain the balance of beneficial organisms in the intestines.

Evaporated milk is whole milk from which 60 percent of the water has been removed. It is then canned and sterilized. Available as low fat (2 percent) and skim, it can be reconstituted with an equal amount of water and used for cooking or drinking.

Condensed milk is similar to evaporated milk, but not usually heat-treated. Sweetened condensed milk contains 40 to 45 percent sugar and is used in candy and dessert recipes.

Non-fat dry milk (powdered milk). This is a completely dehydrated milk product which easily rehydrates in warm water. Instant non-fat dry milk can be rehydrated easily in cold water and can be stored for long periods of time. (It is also available as whole-milk powder.) Dry milk can be substituted for fresh in most recipes and is often used in breadmaking.

Homogenization is a process which disperses the fat globules evenly throughout the milk. Although most milk in the U.S. is homogenized, some dairies still sell unhomogenized milk.

CREAM GLOSSARY

Most cream has been pasteurized, but only half-and-half is usually homogenized to prevent the milk and cream from separating. Look for cream that has not been *ultra-pasteurized*.

Half-and-half. Half cream and half milk, this product contains between 10.5 and 18 percent milk fat. It cannot be whipped, but can be used for a smooth, less-rich substitute for cream in soups and sauces, or in coffee and on cereal.

Light cream (Coffee Cream) contains between 18 to 30 percent milk fat and is used like half-and-half.

Whipping cream or light whipping cream contains between 30 and 36 percent milk fat. It can thicken and enrich sauces and be whipped for use in desserts or mousses for lightness and flavor. It also can be piped onto desserts to decorate.

Heavy cream or heavy whipping cream contains at least 36 percent milk fat. It whips quickly and holds its shape longer. It is used in the same way as whipping cream, but is richer and smoother.

Clotted cream A famous British specialty served with scones and jam, this yellowy cream with a solid butter-like texture contains over 55 percent fat. It is made from unpasteurized milk left to allow the cream to rise to the surface. The cream is then heated so that it sets and can be skimmed off and pasteurized.

Cultured Dairy Products

Cultured dairy products have been used in many national cooking traditions to preserve milk. Adding a variety of bacterial cultures to milk or cream gives body and a unique tangy flavor.

TYPES OF CULTURED DAIRY PRODUCTS

Buttermilk Originally the remaining liquid residue from churning cream into butter. Today buttermilk is made by adding bacterial cultures to fresh pasteurized skim or low-fat milk. This produces a tart, yet creamy-smooth product, drunk as a beverage or added to soups, pancakes, biscuits, cakes, and quick breads.

Sour Cream Made by adding a bacterial culture to pasteurized, homogenized light cream, sour cream has a light, tangy flavor popular in many Eastern European dishes. A low-fat version is available. Sour cream will separate if boiled, so stir into hot sauces at the end of the cooking time, and heat gently just before serving.

Yogurt Recently gaining popularity in the U.S., yogurt has been a fundamental food in the hot countries of the Middle East, Eastern Mediterranean, and India for centuries. It has a thick, tart, custardy consistency. Greek-style yogurt, usually made with sheep's milk, is very popular in Britain and the Middle East. Yogurt, like sour cream, will curdle if boiled, so treat as for sour cream (left).

COOKING WITH YOGURT AND SOUR CREAM

Yogurt and sour cream can be added to soups, sauces, and stews, but handle it carefully.

1 Pour whipping or heavy cream into a chilled bowl. Use a wire whisk or electric mixer to beat until cream begins to hold its shape. Beat into soft peaks when the whisk is lifted from the bowl.

2 For stiffly whipped cream, beat a little longer until stiffer peaks form and a clear trail is left in the cream. *Do not overbeat* or the cream will separate and become granular, eventually turning to butter.

1 Remove the simmering liquid from direct heat and whisk in small amounts of sour cream or yogurt. If sauce cools too much, reheat gently without simmering or boiling.

2 Alternatively, yogurt and sour cream can be stabilized by adding 2 teaspoons of cornstarch per cup/8 oz before adding to sauces. Simmer, but do not boil vigorously or it will curdle.

Butter and Margarine

Butter is a solid fat made by churning cream; it contains about 80 percent butterfat; and 20 percent water and whey (milk solids or proteins) left from the separating process. Salt was originally added to butter as a preservative, but is now used as a flavoring. Its flavor and richness is invaluable in cakes, pastries, biscuits, cookies, and sauces, while it thickens and enriches soups, stews, casseroles, and sauces. Butter is the basis of several classic sauces: Hollandaise, Bearnaise, and Beurre Blanc (white butter sauce). Flavored butters can easily be made ahead and then used to garnish broiled or barbecued meats, poultry, fish, and vegetables. Butter also adds flavor and an appetizing brown surface in frying and sautéeing.

Margarine was invented by a French chemist in 1869. Ironically, the American government set up fierce resistance to it until as recently as WWII. Americans now consume three times as much margarine as butter. A butter substitute, margarine, is made from various vegetable oils, flavorings, colorings, emusifiers, preservatives, and vitamins. Composed of 80 percent fat and 20 percent water, it can be used instead of butter in most recipes, although butter must be used in certain pastries and candy for satisfactory results. Do not substitute soft, diet or whipped margarines, which can contain up to 50 percent water or air.

~RAICHE

~~~ d by pasteurization. It can
~~~ much as 60 percent
~~~ h lower-fat versions
~~~ e. It is used extensively
~~~ ooking. If unavailable,
~~~ de at home (see below).

~~~ to a container and
~~~ ly. Leave in a warm
~~~ 8 hours, until it is
~~~ and a nutty flavor
~~~ tir, then cover, and refrigerate. Reserve 1 cup/8 oz to use as a starter for the next batch.

COOKING WITH BUTTER

When butter is melted for pan-frying, the butterfat separates from the water and whey (milk solids or proteins). In high heat or over a long time, the particles of whey will burn. Clarifying the butter allows the pure butterfat to be removed and used for sautéeing and frying at higher temperatures without burning. Clarified butter is also used for Hollandaise Sauce and as a dip for broiled or barbecued shellfish, asparagus, and artichokes. Indian ghee is a type of clarified butter.

❶ To clarify butter, melt it in a small heavy saucepan over low heat. Tilt pan gently, skimming off all foam from the surface.

❷ Carefully pour clear butter into a bowl, leaving behind milky whey solids; discard solids.

COOKING WITH BUTTER CONTINUED

3 Alternatively, refrigerate melted butter until solid, then scrape off any impurities from the top. Remove separated butter, and discard sediment left on the bottom.

To make *brown butter* for fish or vegetables, slowly heat measured butter *(1 stick/½ cup)* in a small heavy saucepan until golden and foaming and a strong nutty aroma is produced. Remove from the heat, add *1–2 tablespoons lemon juice* and *1 tablespoon freshly chopped parsley*, if you like. Pour over food while the butter is still bubbling. *Black butter* is cooked a little longer until very brown, when other ingredients can be added, and then served at once.

MAKING FLAVORED BUTTER

Easy to make and store, flavored butters can add a special flavor to simple broiled meat or plain cooked vegetables. Use as a topping and spread or cooking medium.

1 Put the softened butter in a bowl and, using a wooden spoon or hand mixer, beat until soft and creamy. Add flavorings and seasonings and blend well.

2 Scrape butter mixture onto a sheet of waxed paper or plastic wrap and shape into a neat log. Wrap and refrigerate until firm. Slice as required and use to top hot foods.

MAKING AND USING KNEADED BUTTER

Kneaded butter (*beurre manié*) is a paste made of equal amounts of butter and flour, used at the end of the cooking period to thicken and give richer consistency and flavor to sauces.

1 In a small bowl, cream softened butter until smooth. Work in an equal amount of flour with a fork until a smooth paste forms. Kneaded butter can be made ahead and refrigerated until needed.

2 Bring sauce or stew to a boil and whisk in small nuggets of kneaded butter to thicken. Continue until sauce is of the desired consistency. Do not continue to cook for long periods; or the kneaded butter will eventually curdle and the sauce will thin out.

FLAVORED BUTTERS

Flavored butters can be made ahead and frozen, then used straight from the freezer. Soften *1 stick/½ cup butter* as above, then flavor as follows:

Parsley butter Add *1 tablespoon lemon* or *lime juice*, *2 tablespoons chopped parsley*. Season with *salt* and *pepper* and serve over meat, fish, chicken, or vegetables.

Herb butter Prepare as above but use *tarragon, chives,* or *cilantro* to replace parsley. Use to top meat, fish, chicken, vegetables, or in soups, stews, and sauces.

Mustard butter Add *1 tablespoon Dijon* or *spicy brown mustard.* Use with broiled or barbecued pork or lamb or on sandwiches.

Garlic butter Add *1–2 chopped* or *crushed garlic cloves.* Use as a cooking medium or to make garlic bread.

Anchovy butter Add *2 tablespoons mashed anchovy fillets, 1 tablespoon lemon juice,* and *freshly ground black pepper.* Use to top broiled or barbecued beef, lamb, fish and as a base for canapés and sandwiches.

Sweet orange butter Add *1 tablespoon confectioner's sugar, 1 tablespoon grated orange zest, and juice.* If you like, add *1 tablespoon orange liqueur.* Use for hot desserts or muffins, pancakes, and quick breads.

Honey butter Add *2–3 table-spoons honey* and spread on bread, pancakes, waffles, and quick breads.

Cinnamon butter Add *1–2 tablespoons confectioner's sugar* and *½ teaspoon cinnamon.* Use as honey butter.

Cheese

Cheese is one of the oldest and most widely used foods. Eaten as a staple food, it is also used as an ingredient in many dishes. Cheese is made by coagulating heated whole, low-fat, or skim milk with an enzyme, causing it to separate into curds and whey. The curds are pressed to form many kinds of cheese; whey is also used to make some cheese, such as ricotta or cottage cheese. Although most natural cheeses are high in fat, protein, calcium, and many other minerals and vitamins, they also contain notable amounts of cholesterol and salt.

COOKING WITH CHEESE

Cheese is generally used in four basic ways: as a flavoring, a topping, a filling, or a dessert. Because of its high fat content, cheese can separate at high temperatures, becoming stringy and oily. When adding cheese to a sauce, remove the sauce from the heat and stir in the cheese until just melted.

For flavor Use hard, aged cheeses which have a high fat content and intense flavor. Aged Parmesan is used to flavor pasta, risotto, and soup; French Gruyère is used in soufflés, gratins, pastries, and sauces; Mature English Cheddar can be substituted for Gruyère or blue cheeses used in salads, soups, and sauces.

For filling Many cheeses are used as fillings or part of fillings, to give extra flavor and body. Ricotta cheese is used in lasagne, feta cheese in Greek spanikoptias, ricotta and gorgonzola fill giant pasta shells. Cheeses are often baked whole, such as Brie in pastry, or breaded and fried. It is often a main ingredient in quiches and tarts.

For a topping Soft or creamy cheeses melt easily and brown well. Mozzarella is often used as a topping for pizzas and many baked dishes, but Brie or Bel Paese could be used. Grated Gruyère is classic on French onion soup, as Cheddar is on Welsh Rarebit. Goat cheese can be broiled to use on salad or toast, or can top pizza instead of mozzarella.

Desserts Most desserts use soft, mild fresh cheeses such as cream cheese for classic cheesecakes, coeur à la crème, cassata, and pashka; mascarpone, a rich Italian cream cheese, is used in tiramisu.

MACARONI AND CHEESE WITH BACON

This recipe uses a classic cheese sauce and a little crisp bacon for extra flavor, but it is just as good without it.

INGREDIENTS
4 slices bacon, sliced crosswise
3–4 tablespoons butter or margarine
³/₄ cup dry bread crumbs
1 onion, chopped
1 tablespoon all-purpose flour
1 teaspoon dry mustard
1¹/₂ cups/12 oz milk
¹/₂ teaspoon salt
¹/₈ teaspoon cayenne pepper
¹/₂ lb shredded mature cheddar cheese (about 2 cups)
¹/₂ lb elbow macaroni

❶ Put bacon into a small skillet and set over medium-high heat. When bacon begins to cook, stir occasionally until it becomes crisp and golden. Using a slotted spoon, remove to a plate and set aside.

❷ Add 1–2 tablespoons butter to the bacon fat and add bread crumbs. Stir to coat and cook about 1 minute until just golden. Set aside.

❸ Preheat the oven to 350°F. Melt remaining butter in a saucepan and add the onion; cook until softened. Stir in the flour and dry mustard. Cook for 2 minutes until a smooth roux forms.

❹ Gradually stir in the milk and bring to a boil over medium heat. Stir constantly until thickened and smooth. Season with salt and cayenne pepper, remove from the heat, and stir in the cheese.

❺ Cook the macaroni in a large pot of boiling salted water until tender. Drain and return to the pot. Stir in the cheese sauce and bacon. Pour into a baking dish, sprinkle the crumbs over the top, and bake about 30 minutes until golden brown on top.

Eggs

Eggs, one of the most nutritious and versatile foods in the kitchen, are served on their own or used as an ingredient in everything from soups to desserts. Eggs provide texture, structure, flavor, and moisture, as well as nutrition. Eggs can be brown or white; color has no effect on quality or flavor, but depends on the breed of hen which lays it.

STORING EGGS

Eggs should be stored in the refrigerator in their carton to maintain maximum freshness and to avoid absorbing other food odors through their porous shells. Choose the freshest eggs for poaching or baking as they hold their shape best; when beating egg whites, choose older eggs, which whisk to a greater volume.

COOKING WITH EGGS

Eggs range in size from small to jumbo, but most recipes use a large egg, about 2 ounces. Although eggs should be stored in the refrigerator, bring them to room temperature before cooking. Eggs are very sensitive to temperature: cold eggs can easily curdle a mayonnaise or cake batter; room-temperature or warm egg whites will whisk to a greater volume. Eggs will continue to cook if left in a hot pan or on a hot plate, so transfer to a serving plate immediately. Use moderate heat for cooking most egg dishes, except omelets.

PEELING MEDIUM- OR HARD-BOILED EGGS

Very fresh eggs are harder to peel than slightly older ones: plunging the cooked eggs into very cold water as soon as they are cooked helps loosen the shell.

❶ Crack the egg around its center, as for separating the egg. Gently roll egg on a work surface until the eggshell is cracked all around the middle.

❷ Peel eggshell away from the white. Holding the egg under cold running water helps the shell come away. Dry gently before using. Store peeled eggs in salted water.

SEPARATING EGGS

The best way to separate the yolk from the white is by using the shell. Avoid breaking the egg into one hand and allowing the white to run through the fingers while cupping the yolk. The white can absorb grease and odors which will inhibit its beating qualities.

❶ Have two bowls ready. Crack the egg as close to its middle as possible by hitting the shell firmly against the edge of a bowl or sharp edge of a counter. Using your thumbs, pull shells apart, allowing some of the white to fall into the bowl.

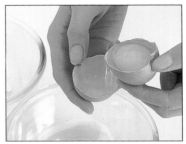

❷ Pour yolk from shell to shell, allowing white to dribble into the bowl. Use one side of the shell to detach remaining white from yolk. Use a shell half to remove any bits of yolk which might slip into whites.

❸ Place yolk gently into the second bowl.

Because they are rich in protein and because salmonella is found in most poultry, eggs can be hazardous if undercooked. Small babies, pregnant women, and the elderly should avoid softly cooked eggs and dishes which might contain under-cooked or raw eggs, such as mousses, soufflés, soft meringues, mayonnaise, etc.

WHISKING EGG WHITES

Beaten egg whites are the basis for meringues and are used to lighten soufflés and mousses. The whites must be free of any traces of egg yolk, oil from hands or bowls, even water. A pinch of salt or cream of tartar added at the start of the beating will help them stiffen. Sugar stabilizes beaten whites and prevents them from becoming grainy, but must be added *after* the whites are stiff. Do not overwhisk or they will be too stiff to fold into the base mixture. Use a copper or stainless steel bowl, as glass and ceramic bowls seem to "repel" the whites and separate them. Plastic can harbor traces of grease or oil, so avoid using it. If in doubt, rinse the bowl with vinegar or lemon juice to remove any impurities, then rinse and dry.

❶ Put whites in a large, grease-free bowl, preferably copper or stainless steel. Begin beating with a large balloon whisk or electric mixer until the whites are "broken" and foamy. If *not* using a copper bowl, add ¼ teaspoon cream of tartar or a pinch of salt to stabilize the whites.

❷ Increase speed and continue beating until whites hold soft peaks when the whisk or beaters are lifted from the bowl.

❸ For meringues, add about three-quarters of the measured sugar, a tablespoon at a time, beating well until the sugar is dissolved (rub a little meringue between thumb and finger – if it is gritty, continue beating). Continue until whites are stiff and glossy.

❹ Sprinkle on remaining sugar (with any other flavorings in the recipe) and gently fold into the meringue. Use as directed.

WHISKING EGG YOLKS

Egg yolks are often whisked separately with or without sugar, sometimes over heat. The whisking increases volume and lightens sauces such as Hollandaise (p.24) or adds air for cakes or batters.

Rinse a bowl with warm water, then dry it. Add yolks and sugar, if directed, and whisk by hand or with an electric mixer until yolks become light in color, thick, and moussy.

FOLDING EGG WHITES

Folding is one of the most important cooking techniques. Because beaten egg whites contain so much air, they are difficult to add to a heavier mixture without losing volume. Folding is a method of combining a light mixture and a heavier one without deflating the lighter mixture.

❶ Do not overbeat egg whites or they will not mix in smoothly and will deflate. To "lighten" the heavier or base mixture, add about a quarter of the beaten whites, and stir them in thoroughly.

❷ Spoon in remaining whites and gently fold in, using a rubber spatula or metal spoon. Cut down into the center of the mixture to the bottom, scooping under and up along one side of the bowl, turning it as you go.

Or, turn the lightened base mixture onto remaining beaten whites. Fold in lightly, cutting down the center with the spatula to the bottom of the bowl, then turning and rolling the mixture over onto itself.

BOILING EGGS

Whatever method you prefer, eggs should never be *boiled,* but gently simmered. To avoid cracking, eggs should be at room temperature. They can be soft-cooked (soft white and yolk), medium or *mollet* (firm white and soft yolk), or hard-cooked (firm white and yolk). Plunge into cold water immediately after cooking time is completed to prevent a greenish-gray ring around the yolk. Hard-boiled eggs can be refrigerated in their shells up to a week.

FOR SOFT- OR HARD-COOKED EGGS
Fill a medium saucepan with enough salted water to cover eggs; bring to a rolling boil. Gently lower eggs into water. Simmer. For soft-cooked eggs, cook 3–5 minutes or to taste. For medium or *mollet,* 5–7 minutes, and for hard-cooked 10–12 minutes.

TO CODDLE EGGS
Put eggs in a saucepan and cover with cold water. Bring to a boil and remove from heat. Cover and allow to stand 6–8 minutes for a soft egg, 8–10 minutes for a hard egg, or to taste. Remove from the water and serve immediately or plunge into ice water and cool. Peel as soon as eggs are cool. This method produces a medium- or hard-cooked egg with a more tender white; it is often used for eggs for Caesar Salad and eggs to be set in molded dishes.

POACHING EGGS

Poached eggs are cooked in just simmering water to produce a moist egg with firm white enclosing a soft yolk. Use the freshest eggs possible; the fresher the egg, the closer the white clings, producing a neat, firm shape. Older eggs will disintegrate as soon as they hit the water. A little vinegar in the water helps the white coagulate. Poached eggs are served on toast for breakfast, in Eggs Florentine, on poached smoked haddock, and in many other dishes.

❶ Begin by cooking 1 or 2 eggs at a time. Fill a deep skillet or wide saucepan with 3 inches water. If you like, add 2 tablespoons vinegar to 4½ cups water. Bring to a boil. Break egg into a saucer or small dish. Using a wooden spoon, stir the water vigorously to form a vortex. Quickly slide the egg into the vortex; this will help shape the egg. Continue stirring and sliding in the eggs. The more experienced you become, the more eggs you will be able to handle.

❷ Reduce the heat and poach in the just-simmering water 3–4 minutes or to taste. Lift egg out using a slotted spoon, and press gently with a finger. It should feel just slightly firm. Remove to paper towel to drain slightly.

BAKED EGGS

Producing what are sometimes called "shirred eggs," is an easy technique to master. Adding extra flavorings or a more elaborate base, such as creamed leeks with smoked salmon, produces an elegant appetizer for a dinner party or a simple lunch or supper.

❶ Butter four ramekins. Sprinkle the bottom with salt and pepper. Break 1 egg into each ramekin and, if you like, pour a tablespoon of cream over each egg, or dot with a little butter.

❷ Cover loosely with foil. Set into a deep skillet or small flameproof casserole. Fill with boiling water. Cook gently on top of the stove or bake in a 375°F oven 5–6 minutes until the white is just set and the yolk still soft. Jiggle one of the ramekins to test the set. Remove from water bath; remember eggs will continue cooking in the dish. Serve immediately.

❸ Alternatively, butter 4 individual baking dishes. Spread a prepared base on the bottom (creamed leeks, chopped tomatoes, or scallions). Make a well in the center of each and break an egg into it. Add a little cream or dot with butter, and cover loosely. Bake as above 10–12 minutes, until lightly set.

SCRAMBLED EGGS

In France, good scrambled eggs are considered an art; gently stirred over low heat to a thick creamy purée, they make an elegant dish garnished with truffles, smoked salmon, or chopped chives. They make a delicious topping for tender pastry, tartlets, or toast. Purists do not add water or milk before cooking, saying it can cause sticking, but it is a question of taste. A spoonful of thick cream or crème fraîche at the end of cooking lowers the temperature and stops the cooking, not to mention adding a delicious richness.

❶ Break 2 or 3 eggs per person into a bowl. Season with salt and pepper, and beat until well blended. Melt 1–2 tablespoons butter over medium-low heat in a heavy saucepan or deep skillet. Add the eggs and cook gently, stirring constantly with a wooden spoon.

❷ Continue stirring as the eggs thicken, until they are soft set and creamy. Remove from the heat and stir until the desired consistency is reached – the heat of the pan will continue to cook them. Alternatively, cook slightly longer over the heat, stir in a knob of cold butter or spoon of cream, then serve.

FRIED EGGS

Fried eggs are often served with crisp bacon or sausages. The fried egg is the centerpiece of the great British breakfast, surrounded by bacon, sausages, tomatoes, mushrooms, baked beans, black pudding, and fried bread. Butter, oil, bacon, or other dripping can be used for cooking.

❶ Melt 1–2 tablespoons of fat in a heavy-based skillet over medium heat. When fat is sizzling, break in 2 eggs.

❷ Fry 1–2 minutes, basting with fat, if you like, until white is firm and begins to crisp around the edge. The yolk should be soft.

❸ For "over easy" eggs, use a spatula to flip each egg carefully. Cook 15 seconds longer, then serve. Alternatively, when whites are just set, add 1–2 teaspoons water to the pan. Cover and cook 2–3 minutes, until done to your taste.

MAKING AN OMELET

Omelets can be rolled or folded, or they can be made flat. They can be filled with a variety of ingredients and make a tasty breakfast, lunch, or supper. A well-seasoned omelet pan is essential, although the newer non-stick pans are excellent. For a 2–3 egg omelet for one person, a 7–8-inch pan is just the right size; 4–5 eggs for two people will cook better in a 9-inch pan.

❶ Break 2 to 3 eggs into a bowl, season with salt and pepper, and beat until well-blended. In a heavy-based omelet pan, melt 1–2 tablespoons butter over medium-high heat, tilting pan to coat well with butter.

❷ When butter is hot and foaming and just beginning to brown, pour in eggs, shaking pan to distribute egg mixture evenly. Cook about 10 seconds, until the bottom begins to set.

❸ Using a metal spatula or fork, gently pull setting egg from the edge of pan to center, tilting pan so that the uncooked egg flows onto the pan base and side. Continue pulling in from the edge until most of the egg is set but the top is still moist and creamy.

4 Sprinkle *1 tablespoon chopped fresh parsley or chives* over the center, then sprinkle over *2–3 tablespoons grated Cheddar or other cheese*. Run spatula around the edge of pan to loosen omelet from the edge. Tilt pan and fold top third of the omelet over onto the center.

5 Hold pan over a warmed plate and begin to slide the lower third of the omelet onto the plate.

6 Tip pan over to help omelet fold onto itself, so that the omelet rolls onto the plate with the edges neatly folded under. If you like, brush the surface with a little melted butter and sprinkle with a few herbs. Serve immediately.

7 Alternatively, for a slightly easier method, proceed as in Step 5 but fold the omelet in half instead of thirds, then slide onto a warmed plate. Finish as in Step 6.

SOUFFLE OMELETS A soufflé omelet is made by separating the yolks and whites, beating the yolks almost to ribbon stage, then beating the whites with sugar to a light meringue. Fold the meringue into the yolk mixture and cook over low heat on the stove or in the oven. The result is sometimes topped with jam or cooked fruit, folded and sprinkled with confectioner's sugar. Soufflé omelets are almost always served sweet as a dessert, although there are savory versions as well.

FLAT OMELETS

Flat omelets are becoming more and more popular. Spanish *tortillas* and Italian *frittatas* are examples of these thick, open-faced, pancake-style omelets. Cut into wedges and serve warm or at room temperature. For an 8-egg omelet, use a 9–10 inch omelet pan with an oven-proof handle; alternatively, wrap the handle well with several layers of foil. Use any favorite filling such as fried onions and peppers, or potatoes, artichokes, shrimp, or ham and cheese.

1 Melt *1 tablespoon butter* and *1 tablespoon olive* or *vegetable oil* over medium heat until hot and foaming. Pour in beaten eggs, shaking to distribute mixture evenly. Reduce heat to low and pull the edges into the center as for a rolled omelet. Arrange filling over the top of the omelet and continue pulling in the edge to allow the raw mixture to flow underneath.

2 Transfer to a 375°F oven and cook 5–7 minutes until set and slightly browned, or slide under a preheated broiler for 3–4 minutes until set.

3 To finish, slide partially cooked omelet onto a large plate. Invert omelet pan over the plate and, holding the two together, invert them again so that the omelet drops into the pan to finish cooking.

Crêpes and Soufflés

Batters are a mixture of flour, liquid (this can vary from milk or water to cream or even beer), and eggs. The proportions differ, depending on its ultimate texture. Batters can be sweet, as for American pancakes or waffles, or savory as for Yorkshire puddings, popovers, or *blini*. They can be thick for fritters and for coating foods like fish, or thin for popovers and delicate crêpes.

MAKING A SOUFFLE

The soufflé is a great example of the egg as a binding and leavening agent. The yolks go into a basic sauce mixture, then the whites are beaten until stiff and light. They are then folded into the basic mixture, and the result baked to a puffy golden brown. Soufflés can be sweet or savory, hot or cold, although the last is not a true soufflé, but more a mousse set with gelatin, presented in the style of a soufflé. All soufflés depend on two techniques; properly beaten egg whites carefully folded into the base mixture, and proper preparation of the dish.

BUSY COOKS

Crêpe and other batters can be made in a food processor or blender. Put the sifted flour, sugar, and salt into the bowl of the food processor fitted with the metal blade. Add the eggs and 1 cup/8 oz of the liquid and process 30–40 seconds until well blended. Strain into measuring jug and stir in the butter. Allow to stand at least ½ hour, then add more liquid if necessary.

MAKING CREPES: FRENCH-STYLE

Crêpes are popular and versatile. They can be filled with sweet or savory mixtures, folded and heated in sauce, or eaten freshly made with a dusting of sugar and a squeeze of lemon juice, as they are eaten on street corners in France. Allowing the batter to stand lets the gluten in the flour relax and allow the maximum liquid to be absorbed. For this reason, a little milk or liquid is often added before cooking to thin the batter to the desired consistency. A non-stick pan makes greasing in between each crêpe unnecessary.

about 18 7-inch crêpes

INGREDIENTS
1 cup/5 oz all-purpose flour
⅛ teaspoon salt
1–2 teaspoons sugar
3 eggs
1⅓ cups/11 oz milk or half milk and half water
4–5 tablespoons melted butter

1 Sift flour, salt, and sugar into a large bowl. In another bowl, beat eggs with 1 cup/8 oz of the liquid. Make a well in the center of the flour mixture and gradually whisk in egg mixture.

2 Draw in the flour from the side of the well to form a smooth batter the consistency of whipping cream.

3 Strain into a large measuring jug.

4 Stir in the butter until blended. Allow to stand ½ hour or overnight, refrigerated. If the batter becomes too thick, thin with a little milk or water.

5 Heat the crêpe pan over medium heat. Brush or spray lightly with a little melted butter or oil. Pour 3–4 tablespoons of batter onto the pan, tilting and turning pan to spread batter thinly and evenly; pour off any excess or fill in any holes, if you like.

FRENCH-STYLE CREPES CONTINUED

6 Cook about 1 minute until golden brown. Using a metal spatula, loosen the edges of the crêpe and shake pan to make sure it is not stuck.

7 Slide the spatula under and flip the pancake.

8 Cook 20–30 seconds longer, then slide out onto a plate. Continue with remaining batter, greasing the pan between each crêpe or as necessary.

9 If using crêpes immediately, stack directly onto each other. To store for later use, put a sheet of wax paper or plastic wrap between each crêpe as you make them. Leave to cool then wrap well, and refrigerate or freeze until needed.

PREPARING A SOUFFLE DISH

The straight-sided ceramic dish is considered classic, since the vertical, fluted sides guide the soufflé upward, but any ovenproof dish will do. Use melted or very soft butter or oil (depending on the recipe) and a pastry brush to coat the dish. Then refrigerate and, when set, butter it again. Some recipes specify coating the buttered dish with bread crumbs, cheese, or sugar.

A collar of paper or foil is not strictly necessary, as most soufflés can sustain their own weight; if used, be sure to butter and coat the paper or foil as directed.

Using a pastry brush, evenly coat the base and side of the dish with butter or oil. Be sure to coat the top inside rim. Refrigerate until set, then butter again and dust with any other coating, if specified.

CHEESE SOUFFLE

Serves 4–6

INGREDIENTS
1 cup/8 oz medium white sauce
4 eggs, separated
1 tablespoon Dijon mustard
freshly grated nutmeg
³/₄ cup/3 oz grated sharp
   Cheddar or Monterey Jack
1–2 tablespoons freshly grated
   Parmesan cheese
1 egg white

1 Prepare a 5–6 cup soufflé dish and set aside. Make a medium white sauce (p.22), reduce heat, and beat in yolks, one at a time, beating well after each addition. Cook, stirring constantly, about 2 minutes, until the mixture thickens slightly. Remove from heat and stir in cheeses, mustard, and nutmeg. Set aside and keep warm, stirring occasionally to prevent a skin from forming.

2 Preheat oven to 375°F. Set a baking sheet on a rack in the lower third of the oven (this helps set the bottom of the soufflé). Beat all 5 egg whites until just stiff. *Do not overbeat.* (In a sweet soufflé, add any sugar.)

3 Stir a large spoonful of beaten whites into the warm cheese base. Using a rubber spatula or large metal spoon, lightly fold in remaining whites until just blended. *Do not overfold* or you will deflate the mixture.

4 Spoon mixture into the dish and gently even the top. Tap firmly on your work surface to dislodge any large bubbles.

5 Bake about 30 minutes, until risen and golden. Shake dish; the soufflé should just tremble, indicating it is still soft in the center. Cook 5 minutes longer for a firm soufflé. Serve immediately. Alternatively, bake in a 400°F oven for 5 minutes, then reduce heat to 350°F, and cook 20–25 minutes longer.

Custard

Custard is a mixture of eggs, milk, sugar (if it is to be sweet rather than savory), and flavorings. There are two types of custard: *stirred custard*, cooked over heat while stirring until thickened, and *set custard*, slowly baked in the oven in a *bain marie* or water bath.

Custards can be temperamental; the most important aspect of cooking is the heat. Custard thickens because the proteins in the egg coagulate when heated. If heated too hot or too quickly, custards will curdle, separate, and start to scramble. Always cook custard *slowly* over gentle heat. Use a double boiler or bowl set over a pan of hot, not boiling water. The custard should thicken slowly; you can feel the consistency on the bottom of the pan. Custard is cooked when the thickened mixture coats the back of a wooden spoon and a clear track remains when a finger is drawn through it. If custard begins to curdle, remove from the heat and beat, or whisk in an ice cube to lower the temperature.

Stirred custard, Crème anglais, or custard sauce is used hot or cold as a sauce for many desserts, as a filling for pastry, and as a base for ice creams, mousses, and many other desserts. It will thicken at 180°F and takes at least 10–12 minutes.

Baked custard needs to cook gently in a moderate oven in a *bain marie* – water bath – which insulates it from direct heat and protects against overheating. *Crème caramel* or flan is probably the most famous set custard. Like a soufflé, when done its center should jiggle slightly, and a knife inserted halfway between the center and edge comes out clean. Set custards are the basis of many quiches and tarts. As a general rule, 1 whole egg or 2 egg yolks will thicken 1 cup/8 oz of milk. The mixture can be made richer by using more yolks or cream instead of milk.

CUSTARD SAUCE

In Britain, Custard Sauce is the traditional topping for many fruit desserts and puddings. A little cornstarch or custard powder is stirred into the beaten egg mixture before adding the milk, stabilizing the yolks and allowing the mixture to be brought to a boil; use about 1 teaspoon per cup of milk.

STIRRED CUSTARD (CUSTARD SAUCE)

INGREDIENTS
2 cups/16 oz milk
1 vanilla pod or 1½ teaspoons
   vanilla extract
4 egg yolks
3 tablespoons sugar

❶ Split the vanilla pod and scrape seeds into a heavy-based saucepan; add the pod.

❷ Pour in milk and bring to a simmer. Remove from heat, cover, and allow to infuse about 15 minutes.

❸ In a medium bowl, beat egg yolks with sugar until lightened and thickened, about 3 minutes. Slowly pour in warm milk, whisking until well blended.

❹ Return mixture to saucepan or top of a double boiler or bowl set over a pan of just-simmering water. Cook over low heat, stirring constantly, until mixture thickens and coats the back of a wooden spoon, leaving a clear trail when a finger is drawn through it. This will take at least 10 minutes.

❺ Immediately strain into a cold bowl, set over ice or ice water. Stir in vanilla extract, if using, and stir custard until it cools slightly. Custard can be served hot or chilled. Stir frequently to prevent a skin from forming if serving cold. The vanilla bean can be washed, dried, and used again.

Fish and Shellfish

Fish are featuring evermore strongly in our daily diet. Bolstered by a strong press extolling its healthful qualities – generally low in fat, and high in protein, vitamins, and minerals – it is the perfect food for today's demanding eaters. While white fish is the lowest in calories and thus the choice of dieters, oily fish can help in the fight against heart disease.

Fish

There are hundreds of species of fish: saltwater fish from the oceans and freshwater fish from lakes, rivers, and streams. Most fish fall into two main categories, depending on their skeletal structure: round fish and flat fish. Round fish generally have plump, thick bodies which can be divided into equal fillets or cut crosswise into steaks or cutlets. These fish tend to have secondary bones which run through the fillets and require removal before cooking. Flat fish such as flounder have a flat central bone with rows of bones along each side. This structure yields 4 fillets and, although they are easy to fillet, the fillets are not of equal size, the top ones generally being larger.

Very large round fish, like tuna and swordfish, have a large central bony spine with four rows of bones radiating out, dividing the fish into quarters. These fish are generally cut crosswise into large steaks which are boneless when separated from the main structure.

The fat content of fish helps determine the most suitable cooking method. Lean fish have firm white flesh and a mild flavor with less than 5 percent fat. Sole, flounder, halibut, snapper, sea bass, turbot, and cod are examples of lean fish which dry out easily. Cooking methods such as steaming, poaching, baking in a sauce or paper, battering or coating before frying are most suitable. Salmon, mackerel, herring, and carp are the oiliest fish, followed by tuna, swordfish, trout, mullet, and monkfish. Oily fish contain 5–50 percent fat, so they are ideal for baking, broiling, pan-frying, or barbecuing.

COOKING FISH

Fish can be cooked by many methods. It can be poached, steamed, pan- or deep-fried, broiled, barbecued, or baked. It can be used in fillings, mousses, pâtés, and terrines. Whatever method you choose, fish cooks quickly, so do not overcook or the flesh will become dry and lose flavor. Raw fish is translucent and becomes opaque when cooked.

CHOOSING AND STORING FISH

Choose the freshest possible fish from a reliable fish market or a supermarket with a rapid turnover. It is preferable to buy and eat high-quality well-frozen fish than poorly handled, old "fresh" fish. When buying frozen fish, select the best quality with all the packaging intact and no signs of ice or blood. Thaw frozen fish in a container overnight in the refrigerator, although fillets and steaks can be cooked from frozen. If cooking from frozen, add a few minutes to the cooking time.

Fresh fish should have a mild, sweet odor and firm, resilient flesh that springs back when touched. The eyes should protrude, not be sunken; the gills should be bright red or pink, not brownish; and scales should be shiny and bright. Fish fillets or steaks should look fresh and moist, not dry, although it's best to buy portions which are prepared at your request.

Fish deteriorates quickly, so keep it in the coldest part of your refrigerator for as short a time as possible. Whole fish keep longer than fillets, and lean fish keep better than oily fish. Arrange dried fillets or steaks in a paper-towel-lined baking dish and cover tightly with plastic wrap. Set over ice in a larger dish, if possible.

Most fish have scales which must be removed before cooking. Although a professional will scale and clean a fish for you, it is an easy skill to master.

IF COOKING A ROUND FISH WHOLE
The fins may be left on to help keep the shape, or just trimmed. Using kitchen scissors or a sharp knife, make a cut along both sides of the dorsal (back) and anal fins, then pull the fin toward the fish head to remove it; snip any smaller fins. Trim off fins behind the gills.

TRIMMING THE TAIL
With the scissors trim the tail into a "V" shape for a neat presentation.

TO SCALE ROUND FISH
Salt your hands for a better grip or hold the tail firmly with some folded paper towel. Put the fish on a board or in a deep sink and, using a fish scaler or back of a large knife, scrape the scales off, working from the tail toward the head. Turn the fish over and scale the other side; rinse the fish and the board.

TO CLEAN AND GUT A ROUND FISH
Use a sharp knife to slit the underside (belly) from the gills to the rear vent (anal fin). Do not insert the knife too far or it may pierce the stomach. (The head may be cut off before gutting if you wish.) Carefully pull out the stomach contents.

REMOVE THE GILLS
Do this either by hooking a finger around them and pulling, or by cutting them out. Rinse the cavity well then, using a teaspoon, scrape along the vertebral column to remove the black blood or kidney. Rinse again and dry well.

FLAT FISH
To trim, use kitchen scissors to trim off most of the fins.
To clean, make a small slit behind the gills and pull out the stomach, then rinse. Alternatively cut off the head by making a "V" shaped cut around it, then pulling the head away and removing the stomach and viscera.

SKINNING FISH FILLETS

Some fish have very tough or oily skins, which should be removed before poaching, steaming, deep-frying, or pan-frying. Most fish skin can be removed with a knife, but catfish, monkfish, sole, and others are best skinned before filleting. Skinning fillets is quick and simple; skinning whole fish may require the assistance of a professional.

TO SKIN FISH FILLETS
❶ Place on a work surface skin-side down, with the tail end toward you. Make a small crosswise cut down to the skin at the top of the tail.

❷ Grip the tail end of the skin and lay the knife against the skin with the blade almost parallel to it. Using a gentle sawing motion, work the knife away from you, separating the skin from the flesh.

CUTTING FILLETS AND STEAKS

Buying a whole fish can often be more economical than buying fillets or steaks. Removing them yourself is easy work with a sharp filleting knife, one with a long, thin, flexible blade. Keep the bones and trimmings (not the skin) of lean fish for making stock (p.21).

Round fish yield two long fillets, one from each side. Flat fish yield four fillets, two slightly thicker fillets from the top and two from the bottom. The fish should be scaled before filleting if it is to be cooked with skin.

TO FILLET A ROUND FISH

❶ Put fish on a board or work surface and cut off the head just behind the gills.

❷ Holding knife parallel to the backbone and beginning at the top end, cut through skin and into the flesh. Cut along backbone to the tail, holding the knife against the bone. You will feel the knife cutting through the secondary pin bones. Turn fish over and repeat with the other side.

❸ Trim any remaining bones from fillets. Use tweezers or a strawberry huller to pull out the little pin bones, feeling along the length of the fillet with your fingers.

TO FILLET A FLAT FISH

❶ Make a curved cut behind the head or cut it off completely. Using the tip of the knife, cut around the outside edge of the fish to outline the two fillets; cut crosswise across the tail.

❷ Locate the center spine. Cut a straight line from head to tail along it. Holding the knife flat against the bones, cut away the fillet using short strokes and pressing against the bone. Turn fish around and repeat.

LARGE FILLETS
Fillets from a salmon, bass, or other fish can be cut into scallops about ³/₈ inch thick for an attractive presentation and quicker cooking. Working toward the tail and holding the knife parallel to the fillet, cut thin, even, diagonal slices.

TO CUT STEAKS FROM A ROUND FISH
Use a large heavy knife to slice the fish crosswise into steaks between 1–1¹/₂ inch thick. The larger center slices are called cutlets. The tail section is too small for steaks but can be divided horizontally to make two fillets.

BONING FISH

Both round and flat fish can be boned and stuffed for an elegant party presentation. In both cases, the head can be left on or taken off, but the fish should be cleaned. If the fish is to be stuffed through the back, it must be cleaned through the gills.

❶ Holding the cavity open, slide filleting knife between rib cage bones and flesh, cutting them loose from the belly edge, working up along the bones to the backbone.

❷ Turn fish onto its belly, opening the flaps like an overturned book. Press along the spine to loosen bone from flesh.

❸ With scissors, cut through the backbone at the tail and head end (if the head remains) and peel it off the flesh, pulling any attached bones with it. Open fish out flat and remove any small pin bones, as for the fillets. The fish is ready for use.

POACHING FISH

Poaching is a gentle method of cooking in liquid which adds moisture and flavor to whole fish as well as smaller fillets, steaks, or cutlets. The poaching liquid – fish stock (p.21), a *court bouillon* (p.19), plain water, or wine – can be used to make the accompanying sauce.

Fish can be poached on top of the stove or in the oven. A large elongated fish pan with a rack for removing and draining the fish is convenient, but not essential.

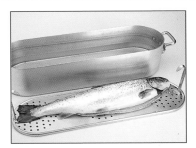

1 To poach a large fish, prepare the poaching liquid and cool completely; use to fill the fish pan or a large casserole. Put the fish on the rack, or set on a long double layer of cheesecloth.

2 Lower fish into the liquid (if using cheesecloth, tie the ends to the handles). Add extra water, if necessary. Bring to a boil over medium-high heat, cover, and simmer gently until done. Drain well and keep warm, if serving hot. Cool, then refrigerate if serving cold.

3 To oven-poach smaller fish, fillets, or steaks, place them in a heatproof greased baking dish. Pour in enough poaching liquid to cover. Cover the baking dish with a piece of greased paper or foil.

4 Bring the liquid to a boil over medium heat, then transfer the baking dish to a 350°F oven and poach until the fish tests done. Remove from the liquid to serve hot. To serve cold, remove from the oven just before the fish tests done, as it will continue to cook in its liquid.

THE CANADIAN DEPARTMENT OF FISHERIES METHOD

This standard method for timing poached fish is a useful guide.

1 Measure the fish at its thickest point. For each inch of thickness, allow 10 minutes cooking time (20 minutes if the fish is frozen).

2 When testing for doneness, if the fish is very thick, remove it from its liquid. Rest the rack angled across the pan. Slide a sharp knife blade into the back of the fish near the dorsal fin. The flesh should look opaque and will not cling to the bones.

Alternatively, if the fish is to be served cold, bring to a boil as directed. Simmer 5 minutes, turn off heat, and allow to cool in the poaching liquid. Do not uncover. The fish will continue to cook in the liquid as it cools. If the fish weighs more than 5 pounds, simmer 10 minutes.

TESTING FOR DONENESS

1 Make a small slit in the thickest part of a whole fish, lifting gently with the blade of a knife. The fish is cooked when the flesh is opaque and pulls away from the bone easily. A large fish will continue cooking when removed from the heat, so if the flesh is slightly opaque near the bone, it will finish cooking on standing.

2 The flesh of cooked fish will feel firm to the touch and offer a little resistance. Raw fish will feel soft, almost mushy.

3 Fish is perfectly cooked when the flesh *just* begins to separate into flakes. If it flakes easily, it will be overdone and dry.

STEAMING FISH

Steaming fish is a simple moist-heat method, favored by the Chinese and those wishing to avoid cooking with fat. Steaming takes about the same time as poaching, but only a small amount of liquid is needed. The liquid should be boiling when the fish is set over it. A very light spray or coating of oil on the steamer rack will keep the fish from sticking.

❶ Arrange fish steaks, cutlets, fillets, or small whole fish on the steamer rack and set over boiling water. Steam, covered, until fish tests done.

❷ Put fish on a plate and set it at the bottom of a bamboo steamer. Place over a saucepan.

❸ Fish can be steamed on a plate without a steamer. Put a small rack, ramekin, or upturned bowl in the bottom of a wok. Fill wok with 2 inches boiling water. Set plate on bowl and steam as above.

❹ Larger fish or fillets can be steamed on a plate or piece of heavy-duty foil set in a roasting pan of boiling water. Cover pan tightly with foil and steam on top of stove or in the oven as above.

SERVING A WHOLE FISH

A whole poached fish is best skinned before presentation. The fish should be skinned while still warm or the skin will be difficult to remove. Broiled or barbecued fish can be served with its crisp skin.

❶ Using a sharp knife, neatly cut the skin behind the head and just above the tail. Slit skin along the backbone and peel it away. Turn and repeat. Remove any fins along the back.

❷ Scrape off dark meat from the middle and discard. To transfer the fish to a plate, use two large pancake turners or spatulas.

❸ To serve, cut the fish down the center and divide into portions. When the top half has been served, slide a server or knife under the backbone to separate it from the fillet underneath. Snap or cut the bone at the head and tail, and lift off neatly, removing it. Serve the second fillet as the first.

PAN- AND DEEP-FRYING

Both pan-frying and deep-frying are excellent ways of cooking fish. Pan-frying uses a shallow layer of fat in a skillet, while deep-frying requires a deep-fryer, saucepan, or wok filled with 3–4 inches or more of oil. Both methods use high heat which seals in the moisture and flavor of the fish. In these methods the fish is usually coated with crumbs or batter.

TO PAN-FRY FISH
❶ Heat just enough clarified butter (p.23) or a mixture of butter and oil to cover the bottom of the pan evenly, over medium-high heat.

❷ When the fat is very hot but not smoking, add fish in a single layer. Cook about 2 minutes per side (depending on the thickness), until golden brown. Drain on paper towels before serving.

TO DEEP-FRY FISH
❶ Fill a deep-fryer, deep saucepan, or wok with 3–4 inches oil. Heat to 375°F and carefully put in the fish. Do not put too many pieces in at one time; this lowers the temperature of the oil.

❷ Fry until crisp and golden, turning once. Remove with slotted spoon. Drain on paper towels.

COATING FISH FOR FRYING

A coating can protect the delicate flesh of fish, keeping in moisture and flavor. Coatings are usually made of bread crumbs, cornmeal, or even oatmeal, or of a batter of flour and egg. Batter coatings are usually used in deep-frying.

BREADCRUMBS

❶ To coat fillets, steaks, or small whole fish: dry fish pieces well and season with salt and pepper. Put flour in a shallow plate and season. Finally put bread crumbs (dried or fresh), in another shallow bowl. Beat 1–2 eggs (depending on quantity) in another bowl. Season. Set aside.

❷ Dip fish pieces (one at a time) first into the flour, turning to coat lightly and shaking off any excess. Then dip the floured fish into the beaten egg, turning to coat all sides.

❸ Dip the egged pieces into the crumbs, pressing to help them adhere, turning and coating on all sides. Gently shake off any excess. Arrange on a plate or baking sheet and refrigerate at least 15 minutes before frying; this helps set the coating.

TO COAT SMALL PIECES OF FISH OR GOUJONS (STRIPS)
Put seasoned flour in a plastic bag and crumbs in another. Toss the small pieces first in the flour by shaking the bag. Then dip pieces into the egg and put into the bag of crumbs, tossing the bag to coat.

TO BATTER-COAT FISH
Prepare batter and allow to rest as recipe directs. Dry fish or pieces very well and dust *very* lightly with flour. Using tongs or fingers, dip one piece at a time into the batter, coating completely. Then immediately lower the fish gently into the hot fat.

BROILING AND BARBECUING FISH

Broiling is an intensive dry-heat method which is best suited to oily fish such as salmon, tuna, trout, or swordfish. Marinating fish adds moisture.

Barbecuing adds a wonderful outdoor flavor to fresh fish. Strongly flavored, oily varieties barbecue best. Fish can be barbecued whole or cut into cubes and skewered. Whole fish should be scored to prevent curling and ensure even cooking.

❶ Use a sharp knife to make 3–4 diagonal slashes on each side, about ¼–½ inch deep. This allows heat to penetrate more quickly. The skin of large fish steaks can be snipped at the back to help prevent curling.

❷ Dry fish well and season as recipe directs. If fish has been marinating, drain well. Place on the broiler pan lined with foil, and brush with butter, oil, or any remaining marinade.

❸ Broil ¾-inch thick buttered or oiled steaks or fillets 3–4 inches from the heat, basting and turning as recipe directs, until done. Barbecue over medium coals 4–5 minutes, depending on thickness, turning once, until done.

❹ To broil leaner fish, add a little liquid to the pan (stock, water, wine, etc.), to provide extra moisture. Baste once or twice to keep fish moist.

BAKING

Baking is one of the easiest ways to cook fish. The fish is placed in an oiled dish, seasoned and moistened with a little liquid – water, wine, stock, or lemon juice – then covered and baked in a 350°F oven. Baked fish remains moist and flavorsome, and because it needs no handling, it is ideal for stuffing. Fish can be wrapped in buttered foil with a few herbs and a little wine or water, then placed on a baking sheet to cook gently until done.

❶ Prepare the stuffing as recipe directs. Fill the cavities of the fish or season the fillets or steaks. Butter an ovenproof dish and scatter over a *small finely chopped onion* or *2 shallots*. Arrange the fish in the dish and brush the tops with *butter* or *oil*. Sprinkle over *3–4 tablespoons lemon juice* or *wine* and bake covered until just cooked.

❷ To bake in foil: butter or oil a long piece of foil. Lay the fish in the center and season.

❸ Sprinkle with *2–3 tablespoons wine*, *water*, or *lemon juice* and wrap the fish, neatly folding the foil like an envelope, allowing air space inside the foil. Set on a baking sheet and bake in a 400°F oven, about 20 minutes for up to a 2-pound whole fish, longer if the fish weighs more.

Almost any fish fillets can be cooked in this way. Try turbot, sea bass, pompano, snapper, or even salmon.

Baking in paper, *en papillote*, is a wonderful way to bake and present fish. The paper turns a golden brown, and the delicious smell and flavor of the fish can be fully savored when the package is opened at the table. This method is surprisingly easy for a smallish dinner party, as it can be assembled ahead, refrigerated, and then placed in a hot oven for about 20 minutes before serving.

FISH FILLETS IN PAPER

INGREDIENTS
2 small carrots, julienned
2 small leeks, julienned
1 medium tomato, peeled, seeded, and chopped
2 slices bacon, diced and cooked until crisp (optional)
4 fish fillets (about 7 oz each) cut in half
2 tablespoons chopped fresh herbs, such as dill, tarragon, chives, or basil
4 tablespoons olive oil
4 tablespoons dry white wine or fish stock
Salt and freshly ground black pepper

❶ Cut four pieces of baking parchment at least 18 inches long and fold in half lengthwise. Cut the open side into a rounded half-heart shape. Open the papers to a full heart and brush each with butter or oil.

❷ Arrange a quarter of each of the vegetables and bacon, if using, on the center of a paper heart next to the fold. Arrange fish fillets on top, sprinkle with a quarter of the herbs, oil, and wine. Season to taste.

❸ Fold the other side of the paper over the filling and, beginning at the rounded edge, fold and twist the edge together as if crimping pastry, to form an airtight package. Tuck the edge under. Repeat with remaining paper packages.

❹ Slide packages onto a large baking sheet and bake in a 400°F oven about 10 minutes, until the paper is browned and puffed up. Slide onto individual plates and allow diners to open their own.

Crustaceans

CRAB AND CRAYFISH

Crab is eaten hot or cold, out of the shell, or *dressed*. In some Chinese dishes, for example, crabs are often boiled or sautéed. There are many kinds of crabs, but the only one eaten shell and all is the tiny soft-shell blue crab, a delicacy found along the east coast of the United States in season.

Fresh uncooked crab should be alive when purchased and refrigerated on a tray of ice until ready to cook, preferably on the same day.

Most crayfish (also called crawfish) in the U.S. is harvested from freshwater rivers and ponds. The white tail meat is used in many dishes, and the heads add richness to Cajun and Creole stocks and stews. You can buy cooked or live crayfish; peeled tails are available fresh or frozen. Live crayfish should smell fresh when purchased and refrigerated immediately after purchase. Use within 2 days.

If crayfish are muddy, soak in cold, salted water for 15 minutes before cooking. Drain and rinse; repeat if necessary. Cook as for crab (see right), boiling for 3–5 minutes until shells turn bright red.

LOBSTER

Lobster is eaten poached, steamed, baked, or broiled, and is served hot or cold. It is one of the most popular shellfish. There are two main varieties of lobster: the *American* or *Maine* lobster has claws and a tail full of meat. *Spiny* or *rock* lobsters have no claws, so all the meat is in the tail.

Whole lobster is sold live or cooked. Lobster tails are available cooked or uncooked, fresh or frozen. Choose the most active of live lobsters and check it feels heavy for its size, with a tail that curls well under. Cooked lobster should have a bright red color and the tail should spring back quickly when uncurled. Cook live lobsters on the same day as purchased or refrigerate on damp paper on an ice-filled pan. Freezing the lobster for 10–15 minutes before cooking will immobilize it completely. (Crab can also be immobilized by this method.)

SHRIMPS AND PRAWNS

Shrimps are the most popular shellfish in the United States, as well as in Britain. The firm, sweet flesh is slightly briny and lends itself to many kinds of preparation. Served hot or cold, they are available year round, fresh or frozen. Refrigerate immediately and cook as soon as possible.

The difference between shrimps and prawns is often blurred. Both are sold by weight, although in the U.S. they are sometimes sold by count.

PREPARING CRAB

Bring a large stockpot of water to a boil over high heat. Add 1 tablespoon salt for each 1 pound of crab or shellfish. Quickly lower crab into water, cover, and return to boil. Reduce heat and simmer about 15 minutes. Drain and rinse under cold running water to cool.

❶ Set the cooked crab on a work surface. Holding the body firmly, twist the legs and claws away from the body.

❷ Use kitchen scissors to snip open the shell on the side of the leg. Pull out the meat with a skewer or crab pick.

❸ Crack the claws with the back of a knife. Discard pieces of the broken shell by hand and extract the meat with a pick or skewer.

❹ Lift up the "apron" (tail flap), twisting it off; discard. To open the body, hold it with one hand. Prize off the top shell with the other hand at the point where the apron was removed.

❺ Discard the "dead men's fingers" (soft gills) from the sides of the body and crack the body into pieces.

❻ Pick out the pieces of meat with a pick or skewer, discarding any pieces of shell or cartilage. The meat can then be eaten cold or used in salads and many other dishes.

REMOVING MEAT FROM CRAYFISH

1 Remove the tail by twisting the head away from the body, to separate the tail. Peel the two uppermost sections of shell from the tail section to expose some of the meat.

2 Turn the tail so underside faces up. With your thumb, press the end of the tail to loosen the meat. Alternatively, snip the underside with kitchen scissors, then loosen.

3 Gently wiggle and pull tail meat out in one piece.

4 Peel the intestinal vein from the back of the tail, starting from the body end and pulling toward the tail.

BOILING AND BROILING LOBSTER

Prepare water as for crab (p.48). Lower the immobilized lobster headfirst into the boiling water. Return water to boiling point and simmer about 20 minutes, until shells are bright red. Drain and rinse under cold running water.

1 To broil: treat as above but cook for 5 minutes. Rinse and dry. Place on a large cutting board, soft underside facing up and, using kitchen scissors, cut soft shell lengthwise from head to tail. Discard all organs, the red coral (roe), and green liver (tomalley).

2 Snip away the sides of the soft shell. Then, using a large heavy knife, cut lengthwise down the body and tail, through the thick back shell.

3 Press open and lay flat on a baking sheet and brush with melted butter. Broil about 4 inches from heat for about 6 minutes, until meat is firm and opaque. Serve immediately with melted clarified butter.

REMOVING MEAT FROM LOBSTER

The cooked shell can be used to present the lobster meat. Pierce the tail to drain the excess water before cutting up the lobster.

1 Put the lobster on a cutting board, hard shell up. Holding firmly with one hand, pierce the shell between the body and tail, cutting down through the tail. Turn the lobster around and cut through the head; you will have 2 halves.

2 Remove and discard the head sac from each side (the roe and liver are edible). Remove the claws and legs by twisting off the body, set aside.

3 Remove the intestinal vein running along the back of the shell and discard.

4 Lift the tail meat out of the shell and set aside.

5 Crack the claws in a few places with a heavy knife or nutcracker. Remove large pieces of shell and pull out the claw meat in one piece, if possible. Repeat with remaining shell.

6 Use skewers to remove meat from the smaller legs.

COOKING SHRIMP AND PRAWNS

To boil fresh raw shrimp, drop into just simmering salted water for 1–3 minutes until shells turn pink. Rinse under cold running water. Drain and dry. Refrigerate until ready to serve.

❶ Twist and pull the head from the body.

❷ Peel away the shell from the body, leaving the end of the tail for a special presentation, if liked.

Fresh or frozen, cooked or raw, peel all shrimp the same way. The heads and shells can be easily removed with your fingers. The tiny brown shrimp are often eaten whole. The shells can be used to make a shellfish stock for soups.

❸ Use a sharp knife to slit the back along the entire curve to remove the intestinal vein. Pull out the black thread with a knife or the fingers.

BUTTERFLYING SHRIMP
To butterfly shrimp for broiling, cup deeply along the back of deveined shrimp without cutting all the way through. Press open to flatten. Butterflied shrimp can be battered and fried.

PRAWN COUNT

The size or "count" is important, because the number of shrimp making up a pound can vary. When calculating how many shrimp are needed per person, remember that two pounds of uncooked shrimp in the shell will yield about one pound of meat after shelling and deveining.

Jumbo shrimp	up to 15 per pound
Extra large shrimp	approx 16–20 per pound
Large shrimp	approx 21–30 per pound
Medium shrimp	approx 31–40 per pound
Small sizes	40+ per pound

Molluscs

MUSSELS AND CLAMS

Mussels and clams are bivalves which should be bought alive and very fresh.

Mussels have a smooth, shiny black shell which is sometimes covered with stone-like barnacles. The "beard," a stringy cord which ties the mussel to its pole, protrudes from the shell. Mussels are usually steamed open in a seasoned liquid, but can be eaten raw on the half shell or used in soups and salads.

There are two varieties of clam. Hard-shell clams include the small sweet littlenecks, cherrystones, and the large chowder clams, minced and used in soups and sauces. Softshell clams include longneck clams – whose necks stick out from the shell – and steamers. These clams have a softer texture than hard-shell clams and are usually steamed, although they are excellent fried or chopped for chowders.

Mussels and clams should be alive when purchased; the shells should be tightly closed or close quickly when tapped sharply. Discard any that do not. Refrigerate them, covered with a damp cloth, and use within a day or two.

OYSTERS AND SCALLOPS

There are two kinds of oysters: native oysters, usually eaten raw, are differentiated by the names of the places in which they thrive. The second type, the Portuguese – despite the name – originates in the Pacific, is more elongated, and has a craggier shell than the natives. Oysters are farmed throughout the United States, Europe, and Australia, and are graded by size, although the grading systems are not uniform. American East Coast oysters are sold as extra-large, extra-select (large), select, standard (small), and very small. In Britain, sizes range from 1, the largest, to 4, the smallest, and in France from 000, the largest, to 4, the smallest.

Although most often served raw on the half shell, oysters can be poached or baked, and are used in soups, stews, and fish dishes. Oysters can be refrigerated on seaweed on a bed of ice for up to one week.

There are two kinds of scallops, the larger sea scallops and the tiny bay scallops. Both types are trawled or dredged at sea; in the U.S., they are shelled and cleaned at sea, as they die quickly out of water. The crescent-shaped coral is often discarded during shelling at sea, but in many places, it is much prized and is eaten with the tender, sweet white meat.

CLEANING AND OPENING MUSSELS AND CLAMS

Do not store mussels or clams in fresh water or they will die.

1 Use a stiff kitchen brush to scrub mussels and clams under cold running water. (Soak clams in sea or salted water, adding a spoonful of flour to make clams expel any sand.)

2 Using a small, sharp knife, pull off beards from shells.

3 To open: hold the hinged end against a heavy cloth in your hand. Working over a bowl, insert a sturdy, blunt knife between the shell halves, working it around to cut the hinge muscle.

4 Twist the knife to prize open the shell. Use the tip of the knife to free the clam or mussel from the shell, allowing it to fall into the bowl with any juices. Refrigerate until ready to use.

COOKING MUSSELS OR CLAMS

Steamed in a little wine with aromatics and sprinkled with parsley, mussels are deliciously sweet. Clams can be cooked in the same way, but are more often steamed open and served with melted butter, or battered and deep-fried.

1 To steam: put a little *dry white wine*, *fish stock*, or *water* into a large stockpot with *2 tablespoons chopped parsley* and any other flavorings as directed in the recipe.

2 Add the *mussels* or *clams*, cover, and bring to a boil. Cook 5–7 minutes until the shells open, shaking the pan frequently. Serve mussels or clams in their shells with their liquid.

OPENING OYSTERS

Discard any loose shell and rinse off any mud which may get into the shell, but do not wash in water or scrub.

1 Hold the oyster flat side up against one palm, covered with a thick cloth. Insert the tip of an oyster knife near the hinge, twisting to prize the shell apart.

2 Slide the knife blade along the upper shell to loosen the muscle; discard the top shell. Run the blade around the edges of the meat. Loosen the bottom. Set the half shell on ice, or tip into a bowl, if using for another dish.

SQUID

Squid, sometimes called by its Italian name, *calimari*, has a firm chewy texture and agreeable flavor. It is usually cut into rings and deep-fried, or simmered in Italian or Greek-style sauces. Whole squid can be stuffed and baked. The ink is used to color pasta and risottos. Squid is also a favorite ingredient in Japanese cooking. Fresh squid should smell sweet and fresh. Refrigerate and cook within 3 days. Squid is also sold frozen and prepared ready for frying. Much fresh squid is skinned and only needs the "quill" removed.

To clean squid, work over a bowl to catch the ink. Firmly grasp the head, then pull the body away from the head, tentacles, and entrails. Discard entrails and reserve the ink sac, if you like. Set aside.

Pull out and discard the long, transparent quill or pen. Peel skin off the body. Rinse and pat dry.

Cut the head away from the tentacles and discard. Rinse the tentacles, dry, and cut or leave whole. Cut the body into rings for frying, chop, or leave whole for stuffing.

Poultry and Meat

Balancing the spread of factory-farming methods and of hormone treatments for leaner meat has been the interest in the traditional and organic rearing of farm animals. The experiences of the last few years have meant that consumers are more aware of quality and taste; all the talent and sophisticated preparation in the world cannot disguise poor ingredients.

Preparing Poultry and Game Birds

Domesticated birds which are reared and fattened for the table are called poultry. Chicken, turkey, duck, Rock Cornish hens, squab, guinea fowl, and geese are the best known. Most poultry is sold fresh and frozen, either whole or in cut-up, ready-to-cook parts. Buy the freshest poultry possible, as it is very perishable. Poultry is highly susceptible to contamination by the *salmonella* bacteria and should be kept refrigerated.

After handling raw poultry, be sure to wash your hands, knives, cutting boards, and any other equipment with which it has come in contact. Raw poultry should never come into contact with other foods, cooked or raw. Frozen poultry should be completely defrosted before cooking.

Fresh poultry should be eaten within 1–2 days after purchase. Remember the sell-by date is the final recommended day for store sale. Properly stored, it should keep for several more days. Remove any packaging, set on a plate, and cover loosely with foil or wax paper. Keep refrigerated. To freeze fresh poultry, buy as fresh as possible, wrap tightly in plastic wrap; then in freezer paper. Defrost frozen poultry overnight in the refrigerator (allow about 3–4 hours per 1 lb). For quick defrosting, set still completely wrapped, in frequently changed cold water. Do not allow the poultry to become wet.

PREPARING WHOLE POULTRY

Some people prefer to wash poultry before using; Kosher chickens are always washed before use to remove any remaining bits of blood.

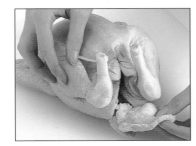

1 Remove any giblets, generally wrapped in paper or plastic, and use within a day or two. Remove any large clumps of fat around the neck and those generally tucked inside the opening of the cavity.

2 Remove any stay feathers or pin feathers, using tweezers or fingers. Rinse the outside and the inside of the cavity under cold running water, removing any bits of blood still remaining. Then dry well with paper towel, inside and out.

TRUSSING A WHOLE BIRD

Trussing, or tying, the bird holds it in a neat shape during cooking. Keeping a neat shape also helps ensure even cooking and, if the bird is stuffed, helps to keep in the stuffing. Trussing can be achieved with a trussing needle and cotton string, or simply by using kitchen string to tie the bird into shape, with or without small poultry skewers. Be sure to remove any string or skewers before serving.

The following method for an unstuffed bird is quicker and easier than traditional trussing and keeps an attractive shape.

FOR AN UNSTUFFED BIRD
1 Set bird, breast-side up, on a board. Pull neck skin taut over the neck opening, tucking it under the backbone. Fold wing tips back and under bird to hold the neck skin.

2 Push legs down and toward the breast to plump it up. Push the parson's nose into the cavity or leave it out, as liked. If the leg knuckles have been left on, tuck them inside the cavity, under the tip of the breast bone.

3 If leg knuckles have been cut at the first joint, bring them together, so the tip of the breastbone is resting on them, and tie together. Cut off any excess string.

TRUSSING A WHOLE BIRD CONTINUED

FOR A STUFFED BIRD
❶ Unfold wing tips. Stuff the neck-end of the bird, then pull the neck skin taut over stuffing. Use a skewer to secure it through the upper part of the backbone. Fold wing tips under the bird.

❷ Fill body cavity with flavorings, such as onion or lemon halves or fresh herbs, as the recipe directs. Then push legs down and toward the breast to plump it up. Tie the legs together with string as on page 53, tucking the parson's nose in or leaving it out, as you like.

❸ If you wish to stuff the body cavity, close the opening with poultry skewers. Depending on the size of the bird, push as many skewers as needed through the skin on each side of the opening.

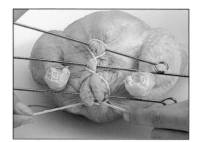

❹ Using kitchen string, lace the skewers together as you would lace a boot. Tie the legs together in front of the opening as on page 53.

POULTRY STUFFINGS
Allow ³/₄–1 cup/1¹/₂– 2 oz stuffing per pound of poultry to be stuffed. Stuff the bird just before roasting.

Spicy couscous Prepare 1¹/₄ cups/8 oz couscous with about 2 cups/16 oz chicken stock and 1 tablespoon butter or oil, adding ground coriander, cumin, and cayenne pepper, to taste. Stir in ¹/₄ cup/1¹/₂ oz dried apricots, chopped, and 2 tablespoons toasted pine nuts. Season.

SPATCH-COCKING POULTRY

Whole birds such as chickens, Cornish Rock hens, guinea fowl, squab, and game birds are ideal for spatch-cocking, or splitting and fattening. Opened up flat, they are ideal for broiling or outdoor barbecuing. Skewering the birds keeps them flat during cooking and makes for easy turning. Marinating spatch-cocked birds adds extra flavor and tenderness.

❶ Cut off wing tips at the first joint. Set the bird breast-side down on a cutting board. Beginning at the tail-end, cut along both sides of the backbone through the skin and rib cage. Remove backbone and reserve for stock or soup.

❷ Turn bird breast-side up and, using the heel of your hand, press down firmly on the breastbone to break it. This will flatten the bird; wipe inside the cavity with a damp paper towel.

❸ Fold wings neatly behind the breast. Make a small slit or cut in the loose skin between the leg and lower part of the breastbone and tuck the leg end into the slit. (The bird can be skewered without this step, but skewering creates a very neat shape.)

❹ Thread a long metal skewer through a wing, into the top of the breast and out through the other wing. Thread another skewer through a thigh, avoiding the bone, through the bottom tip of the breastbone, out through the other thigh.

CUTTING UP POULTRY

Although most poultry is sold in a variety of cut-up pieces, it is much more economical to buy a whole bird and portion it yourself. That way, you can cut the exact number of pieces you want and reserve the bones for stock-making. Most poultry and game birds have similar skeletons, so the following method should be suitable for all.

To cut a bird in half, trim wing tips and cut along each side of the backbone as for spatch-cocking (p.54).

1 Using kitchen scissors, poultry shears, or a sharp, heavy knife, cut through breastbone and wishbone; the scissors or knife will naturally cut along one side, as the breastbone is pointed. You now have two halves suitable for broiling or barbecuing.

2 To cut a bird into 4 pieces, set bird breast-side up on a cutting board. Using a sharp knife, cut through the loose skin between leg and breastbone; the leg will fall away from the body.

3 Cut down to the joint, then twist the leg away from the body to break the joint tendons. Cut through the ball and socket, keeping the tender "oyster," the little pad of meat tucked into the backbone.

4 Hold the top of the breast to stabilize the bird. Cut along the natural break in the rib cage to lift the breast from the lower carcass. Pull the breast and back apart and cut through the connecting joints on each side. Reserve the back for stock.

5 Set the whole breast down on the cutting board. Press firmly against the breastbone to break it. Cut through breastbone and wishbone, cutting breast in half. You now have 4 pieces.

6 Alternatively, remove the legs as in steps 2 and 3. Steady bird on the cutting board and cut down along the breastbone, following the rib cage, until you reach the wing joint; cut through it.

7 The previous step produces 2 boneless breast halves with the wing attached; you have a total of 4 pieces.

8 For 6 pieces, cut each breast section in half at an angle so some breast meat is included on the wing portion. (Leave a little more meat on the lower half.)

9 For 8 pieces, cut the leg portions in half at the joint, separating the thigh from the drumstick. Trim off any excess skin or fat.

BONING CHICKEN AND TURKEY BREASTS

Chicken and turkey breast joints are sold in one piece or as single breasts split along the breast bone. It is easy to remove the bones yourself.

❶ To bone a whole breast, remove any excess fat and the skin, if you like. With a thin-bladed knife, cut through and along one side of the breastbone. Then, holding the knife at an angle, continue cutting down along the rib cage, removing the meat in one easy step. Repeat on the second side; you have 2 skinless, boneless breasts.

❷ To remove meat from a part-boned breast quarter, cut through the wing joint to separate it from the breast; reserve the wing for stock. Remove skin from the breast. Turn the breast over and, using short strokes, scrape meat away from the bone, lifting out the bone as it becomes free.

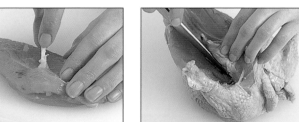

❸ Remove the long white tendon along the underside of the breast fillet as it causes the breast to curl during cooking. Loosen it at one end and pull it out with your fingers. Use the knife to help remove it. The resulting fillet is a chicken *suprême*.

❹ To bone a whole turkey breast crown for stuffing, do not remove the skin. Set breast skin-side down and, starting at the far side, scrape meat away from the rib cage up to the ridge of the breastbone. Repeat on the other side.

❺ Use a knife to free the tip of the breastbone from the meat. Lift it gently away from meat, pulling toward the neck end. Use the knife to scrape meat away from the breastbone, if necessary, being careful not to cut the skin.

CUTTING SCALLOPS

Turkey breast meat makes excellent cutlets for quick cooking. Cutting across the grain provides long, attractive slices which won't shrink and curl when cooked.

❶ Remove the breasts from the bone, as left. Holding a sharp knife at a slight angle, cut long slices crosswise, about ¼ inch thick.

❷ Lay the slices between 2 sheets of plastic wrap. Pound with a meat mallet or base of a skillet to flatten to about ⅛ inch thick.

PREPARING BREASTS FOR STUFFING

Plump chicken or duck breasts make an elegant dish when stuffed.

Using a boneless breast, cut horizontally into the thickest part of each breast, making a wide, deep pocket; be careful not to cut all the way through the meat. Stuff as the recipe directs.

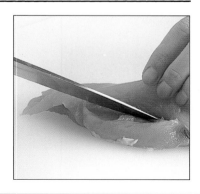

The times given below are a guide. Begin by testing for doneness at the lowest end of the time range. Cook 4–6 inches from the heat source; lower slightly if the meat is coloring too quickly.

Roasting chicken, split in half or spatch-cocked	30–40 minutes
Spring chicken, split in half or spatch-cocked	25–30 minutes
Cornish rock hen, spatch-cocked	25–30 minutes
Guinea fowl, spatch-cocked	25–30 minutes
Squab, spatch-cocked	20–25 minutes
Poussin, spatch-cocked	20–25 minutes
Chicken pieces	30–35 minutes
Boneless chicken/duck breast	10–12 minutes

STUFFINGS – HYGIENE WARNING

Although it has been traditional to stuff the cavity of most poultry, especially the Thanksgiving or Christmas turkey, it is no longer considered absolutely safe to do so. Any existing bacteria resides in the body cavity, and stuffing can inhibit the complete penetration of heat necessary to kill the bacteria completely.

However, if you *do* decide to stuff a bird, be sure the stuffing is prepared ahead and is completely cooled to room temperature. Pack it loosely to allow room for expansion and bake any leftover stuffing in a covered dish alongside the bird. Although stuffing can be prepared ahead, do not stuff any poultry until just before cooking.

Cooking and Carving Poultry

Poultry is the world's most popular bird. Roasting, broiling, barbecuing, pan-frying, sautéing, and deep-frying are all dry-heat methods of cooking suitable for younger, tender birds. Getting the time and temperature right is important to achieve both a crisp, golden skin and moist, tender flesh.

Poultry can be moist-heat cooked using various methods. Braising is generally used for larger, older birds. After browning, a mixture of wine, stock, and vegetables is added and then simmered until tender. Stewing is ideal treatment for mature birds; the French *coq au vin* is a classic example of a chicken stew.

A sauté is a good way of cooking tender, young birds or pieces. First the pieces are browned in butter or oil; then a little liquid added and pieces are simmered over low heat until done. After removing the pieces, the cooking juices are usually reduced or thickened.

Poaching is a good method for cooking older birds, although it also works well for small, tender pieces. The bird can be stuffed or unstuffed, but if it is stuffed, it must be carefully closed so the stuffing does not leak out or the stock seep in.

ROASTING POULTRY

Large birds such as capon, turkey, and goose should be started at a high temperature to give crisp brown skin, then cooked through evenly at a lower temperature to maintain moisture. Do not sprinkle herbs on the outside of the bird at the beginning of cooking, as they may scorch or burn. With the exception of ducks and geese, poultry should be basted with the cooking juices during cooking to help retain moisture.

❶ Rinse bird and dry well inside and out. Before trussing, loosen the breast skin with your fingers by gently easing it away from the flesh.

❷ Spread softened butter mixed with herbs, garlic, or lemon zest on the flesh of the breast and stuff the cavity. Pull the neck skin over tightly and truss as directed (p.53). Spread a little more butter (or oil) on the breast, if desired.

ROASTING POULTRY CONTINUED

TO PREPARE DUCKS AND GEESE FOR ROASTING
1 Truss without adding any extra fat. Prick the skin to allow the fat to drain off. Repeat the procedure twice during roasting.

2 Small game birds should be basted or covered with bacon to prevent lean flesh from drying out.

3 Set prepared bird, breast-side up, on a rack in a roasting pan. Small game birds should be started breast-side down (this keeps the juices in the breast).

4 Roast bird according to the roasting chart on page 59, or as the recipe directs. Cover with foil if the bird browns too quickly. Baste occasionally after the first half hour by spooning over accumulated cooking juices every 10–15 minutes.

5 Put the bird on a carving board, cover loosely with foil, and allow to rest about 15 minutes (longer for larger birds) before carving. Use the cooking juices to make a pan gravy, if you like.

CARVING A WHOLE BIRD

Resting the bird before carving allows the juices to recede back into the flesh, resulting in plump, moist meat. Set the bird on a carving board with a well to catch the juices and remove trussing strings. Spoon any stuffing into serving dish and keep warm.

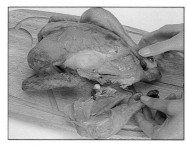

CHICKEN
Using a long knife (or electric knife), cut through the skin between the thigh and body. Continue cutting through to the ball-and-socket joint, then twist the leg away from the body. Cut the thigh and drumstick apart.

TURKEY
1 If carving turkey, slice the dark meat from the drumstick and arrange on a warm serving plate. Slice the darker thigh meat, or leave the thigh whole. Leave thighs and drumsticks whole when carving chicken or other smaller birds.

2 Insert a carving fork into the wing to steady the bird and carve long, 1/8–1/4-inch, slices at an angle, parallel to the rib cage. Cut off the wing. Carve the other side. Arrange the wings and slices on the serving plate with the dark meat.

3 Alternatively, remove the whole breast in a single piece. Then carve the whole breast crosswise into thin slices.

ROASTING TIMES FOR POULTRY

The internal temperature of cooked poultry should reach 165–170°F when an instant-read thermometer is inserted into the bird's thigh.

The following times are for unstuffed birds; allow about 25–30 minutes more cooking time for stuffed birds.

BIRD AND WEIGHT	OVEN TEMPERATURE	TIME (*hours*)
Turkey		
8–12 lb	375°F	3–4
12–16 lb	325°F	4–5
16–20 lb	325°F	4½–5
over 20 lb	325°F	5–6
Turkey breast (whole)		
4–6 lb	325°F	1½–2¼
6–8 lb	325°F	2¼–3½
Turkey drumsticks		
1–1½ lb	325°F	1¼–1¾
Chicken		
2½–3 lb	375°F	1–1¼
3½–4 lb	375°F	1¼–1¾
4–6 lb	375°F	1½–2½
Capon		
5–7 lb	325°F	1¾–2
Rock cornish hens		
1–1½ lb	375°F	1–1¼
Whole duckling		
3½ lb	375°F	1¾–2¼
Goose		
8–10 lb	350°F	2½–3
10–12 lb	350°F	3–3½
Squab		
12–14 oz	370°F	40–50 min.

BROILING AND BARBECUING

Broiling and barbecuing are popular methods of cooking all types of poultry. Spatch-cocked small birds or cut-up pieces are ideal. Marinating beforehand helps flavor the meat as well as tenderize it, but is not essential.

Prepare a simple Asian-style marinade by combining ¼ cup/ 2 fl oz soy sauce; 1 tablespoon sesame oil; grated zest and juices of 1 lemon, lime, or orange; 2–3 chopped scallions; a tablespoon of chopped fresh ginger; a tablespoon of chopped cilantro; and a little water to dilute.

❶ Put spatch-cocked birds or pieces in a glass or stainless-steel dish and add the marinade. Leave at least 1 hour or overnight. Prepare an outdoor charcoal fire or preheat the broiler. Line a broiler pan with foil and arrange the drained birds or poultry pieces on the pan, or on an oiled rack over the fire.

❷ Broil or barbecue about 4–6 inches from the heat, about 20 minutes for a spatch-cocked bird or 10 minutes for poultry pieces, turning once and basting with the marinade halfway through cooking. (If not using a marinade, brush the poultry with a little oil and season with salt and pepper.)

STIR-FRY

Poultry is a popular choice for stir-frying. Use tender pieces cut into small even sizes, so they cook evenly.

❶ Heat a wok or large skillet over high heat. Add 1–2 tablespoons oil and swirl to coat the bottom and side of the wok. Add any flavorings as directed (garlic, ginger, scallions); stir-fry 30 seconds.

❷ Add cut-up poultry pieces and any marinade; cook, stir-frying until lightly colored, 1–2 minutes.

❸ Add any other ingredients and continue as recipe directs.

FRYING CHICKEN

Fried chicken with its crisp brown coating and tender, juicy meat is a flavorsome way of preparing chicken. Dry the chicken well, since any moisture will cause the oil to spatter. Chicken pieces can be battered or coated with crumbs.

TO PAN-FRY WITHOUT COATING

1 Heat a mixture of oil and butter in a large, heavy-based skillet over medium-high heat. Add the pieces, skin-side down, working in batches, if necessary.

2 Fry, turning to brown well on all sides, until cooked through. This will take at least 25 minutes. Remove the breast pieces before the thighs and drumsticks, since they cook more quickly. Drain on paper towels.

TO DEEP-FRY

1 Flour the pieces lightly, then dip into a mixture of beaten egg and milk. Coat lightly with seasoned flour, cornmeal, or crumbs. Refrigerate 20 minutes to set the coating. If battering, dip the pieces into the batter and immediately lower into the hot oil.

2 Fill a deep-fat fryer or deep saucepan or casserole with 3–4 inches oil. Heat over medium-high heat to 365°F; a small cube of bread tossed into the oil will brown in just under a minute. Using tongs or a pancake turner, carefully lower the pieces into the oil; do not overcrowd or the temperature of the oil will drop. Fry until deep golden and cooked through, turning to color evenly, 25–30 minutes.

3 Drain on paper towels. Keep warm in a low oven while frying any remaining pieces.

POT ROASTING

Pot roasting is a general term for cooking in a covered casserole. The whole bird is generally browned first, then cooked in its own juices or in a little stock, together with root vegetables like onions, potatoes, and carrots. The bird can be stuffed or unstuffed, but if stuffed, be sure it is well sealed to avoid any leakage.

1 Heat 2–3 tablespoons vegetable oil in a heavy-based casserole just big enough to hold the bird and any vegetables. Brown the bird, turning to color on all sides.

2 Add about 1 cup/8 oz stock and any flavorings – such as a bay leaf and a few fresh thyme sprigs – and any vegetables. Bring to a boil over medium-high heat, cover, and transfer to a preheated 350°F oven.

3 Cook for about 1¼ hours, or until the birds are cooked through. The juices will run clear, and the legs will move freely in their sockets when wiggled.

Carefully place the bird on a cutting board. Remove the strings and discard. Spoon the stuffing into a dish. Meanwhile, reduce the juices over high heat, scraping up any bits on the bottom of the pan. Strain the gravy over the bird or serve separately.

GAME BIRDS

Care must be taken not to let the meat dry out. For roasting, birds should be barded or covered with bacon. Many game birds are traditionally eaten quite pink, so the breast remains undercooked and juicy.

ROASTING TIMES

Small game birds
Teal, woodcock, snipe, partridge, pigeon, quail, and red grouse

450°F   15–30 minutes

Medium game birds
Blackcock, pheasant, mallard, and other wild duck

400°F   per pound – rare: 15 minutes medium: 20 minutes

Large game birds
Wild turkey, sage grouse, geese

425°F   per pound – rare: 12 minutes well done: 15 minutes

Choosing and Preparing Meat

In general, look for well-cut, well-trimmed meat; smaller cuts, such as steaks and chops, should be evenly cut or sliced so they cook at the same rate. Flesh color should be clear but not bright, with no gray or yellow tinges and no dry edges. Beef should be well marbled – that is, lightly streaked with flecks of fat. Exterior fat should be creamy white, feel firm, and have a soft, waxy texture. All meat should smell fresh and look moist. Yellow fat can indicate old meat.

Select the cut most appropriate to the cooking method you are using. Tender cuts from the loin, fillet, and saddle (the back of the animal) are most suitable for dry-heat cooking methods such as roasting, broiling, or frying. Less tender cuts from the top of the rump, flank, or breast are more suitable for pot-roasting or braising, both moist-heat cooking methods.

As a general rule, allow about 6–7 ounces of boneless lean meat per person. For meat on the bone such as a rib roast, allow about 8–12 ounces per person, and for very bony meats such as spare ribs, 1 pound per person is needed. The preceding is very much a personal choice.

Store meat on a plate in the coldest part of the refrigerator. The temperature should be 30–35°F. Loosely cover precut meats; wrapping tightly encourages the development of bacteria. Store prepackaged meats in their containers. Never allow any meat to come into contact with other foods, raw or cooked. Larger cuts will keep longer than smaller cuts and pieces: beef and lamb will keep slightly longer than pork or veal. Ground meat should be cooked within 2 days if prepacked, one day if bought loose. Frozen meat should be thawed overnight in a refrigerator, not at room temperature or even under cold running water.

All meats harbor bacteria. Bacteria increase rapidly at room temperature and can cause meat to spoil. Refrigeration slows down the process and freezing stops it, although bacteria will begin to multiply when the meat is thawed. Cooking at high temperatures kills the bacteria, but they can still be present in lightly-cooked meat. Pregnant women, children, the elderly, and people with serious health conditions should avoid raw or lightly cooked meats.

Always wash your hands, knives, cutting boards, and any other utensils used to prepare raw or cooked meats. Ideally, meat should be cooked thoroughly to kill all bacteria. A meat thermometer inserted in the thickest part of a joint should read at least 160°F, although some bacteria may still survive at this temperature. Rolled or stuffed roasts may contain bacteria within, so extra care is needed to make sure the heat penetrates adequately to kill the bacteria. Once cooked, cool leftover meat as quickly as possible, then refrigerate.

SUITABLE CUTS FOR COOKING METHODS

METHOD	TYPE OF MEAT	CUT OF MEAT
Roasting (dry-heat)	Beef	Rib (fore), prime rib or wing rib, short rib, tenderloin or fillet, sirloin, and topside
	Veal	Shoulder, loin, fillet, breast, topside, and neck
	Lamb	Shoulder, best end of neck (crown roast), saddle, loin, breast, leg
	Pork	Shoulder (spare rib), hand and spring, blade, loin, tenderloin (fillet), leg, spareribs; ham, collar and hock
Pot-roasting	Beef	Brisket, top ribs, sirloin, topside, chuck, flank, rump, braising steak
	Veal	Shoulder, best end of neck, middle-neck cutlets, breast
	Lamb	Shoulder, middle neck, cutlets, breast, loin, leg
	Pork	Shoulder (spare rib), loin, tenderloin (fillet). Ham joints, collar and neck
Stewing	Beef	Neck, chuck, shin, flank, leg, skirt
	Veal	Neck, shoulder, breast, knuckle (osso buco), stewing veal, or pie veal
	Lamb	Middle neck, shoulder, breast, chump chops
	Pork	Spare rib, tenderloin, loin

SUITABLE CUTS FOR COOKING CONTINUED

METHOD	TYPE OF MEAT	CUT OF MEAT
Pan-frying	Beef	Tournedos, sirloin steak/porterhouse, rump steak, T-bone steak, entrecote, chateaubriand, hamburgers
	Veal	Cutlet, loin chops, chump chops, scallops, fillet steaks (medallions)
	Lamb	Cutlets, boneless cutlets, loin chops, chump chops, leg steaks, tenderloin (fillet)
Pan-frying	Pork	Loin chops, spare-rib chops, cubes or slices of tenderloin; Bacon, ham steaks and chops, sausages
Broiling	Beef	Tournedos, sirloin steak/porterhouse, rump steak, T-bone steak, hamburgers
	Veal	Cutlets, boneless cutlets, loin chops, chump chops, leg steaks, tenderloin
	Pork	Loin chops, spare-rib chops, tenderloin; bacon, ham steaks and chops, sausages
Stir-frying	Beef Veal Lamb Pork	Strips of tender beef steaks, strips of veal scallops, strips of lamb and pork tenderloin or leg

PREPARING MEATS

Even meats prepared by the butcher or bought ready-to-eat in the supermarket may need extra trimming before cooking. As a general rule, remove as much exterior fat as possible. Use a sharp knife to remove any rind or skin and thick fat from the surface of the meat. A thin layer (about $\frac{1}{8}$ inch) can be left on large roasting pieces. Leave a little fat on steaks or chops for broiling, but slash the edges or snip with kitchen scissors at $\frac{1}{2}$-inch intervals to prevent curling during cooking.

When trimming meats, trim the fat and any gristle from bones and wrap with foil to prevent burning. Cut out any sinews or tough connective tissues, sliding the point of a sharp knife underneath to loosen it, then cut away.

TO CHINE A LARGE CUT
Remove or loosen the backbone where it is joined to the ribs. Any cut such as rib roasts, loin roasts, best-end of neck, and even small racks of lamb should be chined with a meat saw; it is best to ask your butcher to do this. Supermarket cuts are usually prepared in this way, to allow for easier carving. If you like, remove the backbone completely.

TO BARD A ROAST
The technique of barding is usually done to protect a large cut which is to be roasted. Cover the meat (or game) with thin slices of beef or pork fat, or bacon, and tie in place with string. As the meat cooks, the fat or bacon slowly melts and bastes the meat, keeping it moist. Remove and discard the fat before serving; the crisp bacon can be served alongside the meat if you like.

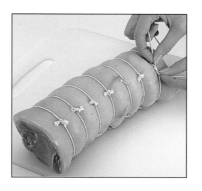

TO TIE A BONED PIECE OF MEAT
Large cuts which can be bought boned for stuffing or easier carving need to be tied into a firm, neat shape before cooking. After stuffing or seasoning, reshape the meat into a neat roll. Use string to tie the meat at 1-inch intervals before roasting or pot-roasting.

Avoid using wooden cutting boards which are difficult to clean or disinfect. White, nonporous chopping boards can be scrubbed with hot water and disinfected or put through the dishwasher.

TENDERIZING MEAT

Meat can be tenderized by pounding, scoring, or marinating. These techniques break down the fibers in meat, rendering them more tender and adding flavor.

VEAL SCALLOPS OR THIN STEAKS
❶ To pound thin cuts such as veal scallops or thin steaks, lay the meat between 2 sheets of plastic wrap or wax paper; pound with a meat mallet, rolling pin, or bottom of a heavy-based pan.

❷ Use a sharp knife to score the meat lightly in a diamond pattern. This technique literally cuts through many of the tougher fibers.

CUTTING THE TENDERLOIN/FILLET: BEEF

❶ Cut and trim away as much fat as possible, then cut away the "chain muscle" which lies to the side of the main meat. Use it for stewing or grinding.

❷ Pull out the "silverskin" or tight tissue coating which surrounds the meat. Slide the point of a knife under it and scrape away from the meat, leaving the meat completely clean beneath.

FOR ROASTING WHOLE
Fold the tapered end under to make an even shape or cut off 4–5 inches from the tapered end to make an even shape; use the trimmed end for kabobs or strogonoff. If you like, bard and then tie the tenderloin.

TO CUT INTO STEAKS
Trim off the end as above. Beginning from the thick (neck) end, cut about four 1½-inch thick slices; these are called *Tournedos* or *Filet Mignon*. Cut the center section into two 5-inch pieces for *Chateaubriand* (these are roasted at high heat); cut the remaining meat into 1-inch fillet steaks.

TENDERIZING MEAT USING MARINADES

Marinades can be cooked or "raw," but usually contain a mixture of oil; an acid such as vinegar, lemon, or lime juice; and herbs and flavorings. The acid acts to tenderize the meat; the oil acts as a lubricant, and of course the herbs add flavor. If the marinade is cooked, such as a robust red wine marinade for beef or venison, allow it to cool completely before adding to the meat.

Large pieces of beef and game can be marinated in a cooked marinade for up to 3 days, small cuts for a day, while more delicate meats such as veal or liver should only be marinated for 1–2 hours. Pork marinades often use sweet and sour flavors or barbecue sauces.

Lay the meat or pieces of meat in a non-corrosive dish. Pour in the marinade and turn the meat to coat well. Cover and leave to marinate several hours at room temperature, or overnight in the refrigerator. The time required depends on the meat, the cut, and how much tenderness and extra flavor is wanted. Turn the meat every few hours.

CUTTING MEAT FOR STEWS

To cut cubes of meat for stewing, start with a large piece of chuck steak or braising steak. Trim away as much fat and gristle as possible. Cut the meat into 2-inch cubes.

GRINDING MEAT

It is easy to grind or chop your own meat at home to give absolute freshness. Any tender cut of beef, pork, veal, or lamb can be ground for a variety of dishes.

USING A MEAT GRINDER
1 Trim the meat well, then cut into 1-inch cubes.

2 Feed into the grinder, fitted with the coarse blade. This gives the most uniform texture. For finer meat, use the fine blade.

CHOPPING BY HAND
Trim the meat as above and cut into cubes. Using a large chef's knife, chop the meat until you have the desired consistency.

BUSY COOKS

1 If using a food processor fitted with the metal blade, trim the meat of all fat, gristle, and sinews. Cut into 1-inch cubes, put into the processor, and using the pulse button, process 2–3 times.

2 Remove the cover to check the consistency and scrape the side of the bowl. Pulse once more if necessary, but do not overprocess, since it can easily purée the meat.

BONING A LOIN OF LAMB FOR ROASTING

1 To bone a lamb loin or saddle (double loin) for roasting, set the trimmed loin skin-side up on a work surface and trim the "fell" (the papery layer of connective tissue) from the surface. Trim the surface fat to about ¼ inch.

2 Turn the saddle or loin over and trim as much fat from the underside as possible.

3 Starting from the center of the backbone, slide the knife between the tenderloin and the rib bones. Cut the flesh away from the bone, but leave the meat attached to the flank. Continue until all the rib bones on one side have been freed. Repeat on the other side.

4 Slide the knife under the back and rib bones, separating the meat from the ribs and backbone.

5 Using your hands, pull out the backbone from the meat, leaving the loins intact.

6 Roll the flank flaps toward the center from each side. Tie the roast with kitchen string at 1-inch intervals. The meat is ready for roasting.

CUTTING VEAL SCALLOPS

Veal scallops are the most popular veal cut. The best scallops come from the fillet end of the leg, but they can also be cut from the best end of neck or shoulder.

1 Cut all fat and sinews from a piece of leg fillet at least 5 inches wide. Holding a long, sharp knife diagonally at an angle, cut across the meat into slices about $1/8$–$1/4$ inch thick.

2 Lay the slices between 2 sheets of plastic wrap. Pound to flatten and tenderize, being careful not to make holes or tear the meat.

CUTTING NOISETTES FROM A LOIN

1 To cut lamb noisettes from a loin, remove the loin meat by cutting down along the backbone and along the ribs. Pull out the bone. Trim the tenderloin evenly, leaving a thin layer of fat. Roll up the loin and tie at intervals with string.

2 Using the string as a guide to size, cut the tenderloin into small noisettes $3/4$–1 inch thick.

BONING, ROLLING, AND BUTTERFLYING A LAMB LEG

Partially boning a leg of lamb makes for much easier carving. Boning it completely leaves it free for stuffing and rolling, or for butterflying – opening up flat for broiling, roasting, or barbecuing. Trim off the fell and as much exterior fat as possible. To remove the pelvic bone – made up of the aitch bone and hip bone – set the leg on a cutting board with the pelvic bone facing up.

1 With a sharp boning knife, cut around the exposed ball and socket joint between the hip bone and main leg bone. Free it from the meat. Cut completely around the pelvic bone and remove it.

2 Beginning at the top of the exposed leg bone, cut down along the bone through the meat, from the top to the knee joint. Using short, quick strokes, curl and scrape the meat from the bone all the way around.

3 Continue cutting along the length of the shank bone, cutting and scraping the meat away; the bone should be almost free. Lift out the leg bone and cut around the knee joint, freeing the meat completely. Remove as many tendons as possible by scraping them away from the meat.

TO ROLL THE MEAT FOR ROASTING Season, and if you like, spread the stuffing along the center. Roll as neatly as possible, tucking in the small end piece. Tie at 1-inch intervals. The boned leg is ready for roasting.

TO BUTTERFLY THE LEG
Lay the meat flat on the work surface, boned side up. Holding the knife parallel to the meat, slit open the thick upper portion to create a slab of even thickness. Trim any remaining fat or tendons.

To keep the meat flat during cooking, thread 2 or 3 long metal skewers through at the widest part. This also makes the meat easier to turn.

Dry-heat Cooking Methods

There are two general types of cooking methods: dry heat and moist heat. Dry heat methods include roasting, broiling, grilling, baking, sautéing, pan- and deep-frying. Foods cooked by dry heat methods have a richer flavor caused by browning, which caramelizes the natural sugars in the meats or other foods. Cooking by dry heat involves applying heat directly or indirectly.

ROASTING MEAT: ROAST PRIME RIB OF BEEF WITH PAN GRAVY

The fierce dry heat of oven roasting is perfect for tender cuts of most meats. Leaner meats can be barded or marinated. Bring meat to room temperature before roasting so that it cooks evenly.

Cook smaller roasts like lamb racks or beef tenderloin at high temperatures for good surface color; large cuts cook better and shrink less if cooked at a lower constant temperature.

INGREDIENTS
3 rib-prime rib roast, backbone chined, about 10 lb
salt and freshly ground pepper
1 large onion, quartered
2 carrots, cut into 2-in pieces
1 stalk celery, cut into 2-in pieces
1½ cups beef stock

❶ Preheat oven to 350°F. Brush a roasting pan with oil, then rub the surface of the meat with remaining oil. Season meat with salt and pepper.

❷ Put cut-up vegetables in the roasting pan. Set the meat on top, fat side up. Roast beef for 20 minutes per pound until a meat thermometer inserted in the thickest part of the meat reads 135°F for medium-rare beef.

❸ Transfer beef to a carving board and cover with a foil tent. Allow to rest for 15–20 minutes.

MAKING PAN GRAVY

❶ To make pan gravy, spoon off all but 1–2 tablespoons of fat from the pan drippings. Set the pan over medium-high heat and, when the juices begin to boil, sprinkle in the flour. Using a wooden spoon, scrape up the browned bits on the bottom of the pan until a smooth paste or "roux" forms.

❷ Gradually pour in stock, stirring constantly until a smooth gravy is formed. Allow to come to a boil, then season with salt and pepper, and simmer about 5 minutes. Strain the gravy into a gravyboat and keep warm.

TESTING FOR DONENESS

Large roasts will continue cooking for up to ten minutes after being removed from the heat.

USING A MEAT THERMOMETER
Provides the most reliable check. Insert the thermometer into the thickest part of the meat, being careful not to touch any bones. An instant-read thermometer can be inserted at the end of the cooking time to verify the temperature.

USING A METAL SKEWER
Insert the skewer into the thickest part of the meat, leave for 30–40 seconds. Pull out the skewer and feel it: if still cold or cool, the meat is not done; if warm, the meat is rare; if hot, it is cooked.

CARVING A RIB ROAST

All roasted meats should rest in a warm place before carving; tenting with foil helps to keep the meat warm. Resting allows meat to relax and reabsorb juices which would otherwise be lost when the meat is carved. A large cutting board with a well to collect the juices is ideal. Meat cuts vary, but most should be cut across the grain; the more tender the meat, the thicker the slices can be.

1 Holding the meat with a carving fork, slice horizontally along the rib bones to remove them completely.

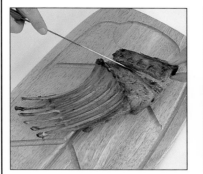

2 Place the meat boned side down and slice crosswise into thick or thin slices. Alternatively, slice downward between the ribs, leaving a rib on each alternate slice.

MEAT ROASTING TIMETABLE

The following times are for meats started at 450°F for 15 minutes, then finished at 350°F. Larger cuts are better roasted at a lower constant heat.

MEAT	DEGREE OF DONENESS	THERMOMETER READING	MINS. PER LB
Beef	Rare	125–130°F	12–15
	Medium	135–140°F	15–18
	Well Done	145–160°F	18–20
Veal	Well Done	160°F	18–20
Lamb	Rare	130–135°F	15
	Medium	140–145°F	15–18
	Well Done	160°F	18–20
Pork	Well Done	160–165°F	20–25

A good carving knife is an essential piece of equipment in every kitchen. The stainless steel knife has a fine edge, requires moderate sharpening, and needs no polishing. Ideally, knives should never be kept in a drawer unless covered with a plastic or leather sheath; they are best held in a block wood holder designed for the purpose, in a specially fitted drawer, or on a wall-hung magnetic rack.

CARVING A RACK OF LAMB

1 Set the meat on a cutting board with the backbone on your left. Remove the chined bone.

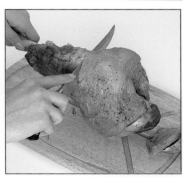

2 Holding the rack with the ribs in the air, carve downward with the knife, cutting cleanly between each rib.

CARVING A LAMB LEG

1 Set the meat on the cutting board with the shank bone on your left side. Cut off a few slices from the thin side, then set the leg on the flat surface to balance it.

2 Starting at the shank end, slice down to the leg bone until you reach the other end. Holding the knife parallel to the leg bone, cut under the slices to release them.

PANBROILING AND SAUTEING

Panbroiling and sautéing are dry-heat methods using small amounts of fat in an open pan. As with other dry-heat methods, use tender cuts such as steaks, scallops, slices of liver, and hamburgers. Use a heavy-bottomed pan and oil or clarified butter, as ordinary butter can burn. Sautéing uses slightly less vigorous heat and only a small amount of oil. After cooking, the juices in the pan can be deglazed to make a simple sauce.

① Heat 2 tablespoons of oil or half oil and half butter in a heavy-based skillet, large enough to hold the meat without crowding, over medium-high heat. Season the meat and add to the pan.

② Fry until well-colored on one side, then turn to brown on the other. For pork chops or other meats which require complete cooking, lower the heat after the initial browning to allow the meat to cook through without burning.

TO DEGLAZE PAN JUICES

During panbroiling the meat exudes flavorful juices, and brown crusty bits form on the bottom of the pan. Adding wine, alcohol, vinegar, cream, stock, or water to dissolve the sediments is called *deglazing*. This is a quick easy way to make a simple sauce, add more flavor to stews, and make gravies for roasted meats.

① Remove cooked meat from the pan and keep warm. Tilt the pan and, using a spoon, scoop off as much fat as possible; this is called *degreasing*. Add any ingredients called for in the recipe, such as garlic, shallots, onions, or mushrooms, and stir.

TESTING PANBROILED MEATS FOR DONENESS

Cooking time depends on the meat, the thickness of the cut, and the temperature. Pressing the meat with your fingers can give an indication of doneness; the more well-done the meat, the more resistance it will offer.

Using your index finger, press firmly against the center of the cut. If the meat is very rare or underdone, it will feel soft, offering almost no resistance. If it is cooked medium-rare, it will offer a little resistance, but will feel slightly soft inside with a few droplets of juice forming on the surface. Well-done meat will feel very firm to the touch and have considerable juice on the surface. You will soon learn to judge the degree of doneness you require.

② Return pan to the heat and pour in the liquid as directed by the recipe. Bring to a boil, stirring and scraping up all the sediment from the bottom of the pan.

③ Boil for 1–2 minutes or until the liquid is thickened or syrupy. Add any remaining ingredients, if the recipe indicates, and season. Serve over the pan-fried or sautéed meat.

MAKING MEAT SAUTES

Not to be confused with pan-broiling and sautéing meats, a meat sauté is a dish browned in oil or butter, then covered to cook gently in its own juices. Pork and veal cutlets, veal scallops, and pork tenderloin, as well as other stewing cuts of veal and lamb, are juicy cuts suitable for sautés. The meat must be cut in even-sized pieces which can then be seasoned and dusted with flour before browning. Add a little deglazing liquid at the end of cooking, but the meat should never be covered with liquid.

① Trim the fat and connective tissue from a pork tenderloin or other meat. Holding the knife at an angle, cut the tenderloin into 4 or 6 equal-sized scallops. Seasoned with salt and pepper and dust with flour.

② Heat 2–3 tablespoons vegetable oil, or half oil and butter, or clarified butter, in a deep, heavy-based skillet over medium heat. Add the pieces of meat (do not crowd them) and brown gently, turning to color evenly. *The pan should be covered during sautéing.*

③ Drain any excess fat and, if recipe directs, add vegetables such as baby onions, mushrooms, tomatoes, or zucchini. Cover the pan and simmer until the vegetables are tender, shaking the pan frequently or turning the vegetables to color evenly.

④ When the meat is fork-tender, add about ¹⁄₂ cup/4 oz liquid such as wine, stock, or cream to deglaze the pan (p.68) or as recipe directs. Season before serving.

BROILING MEATS

Broiling exposes food directly to the heat (flame or element), so only the best-quality, tender, well-marbled cuts of meat should be used. A little exterior fat is necessary to keep the meat moist, but too much may cause the broiler to flame up and burn the meat. Trim as much connective tissue as possible, since it will cause the meat to toughen. If broiling veal or pork, cook at a slightly lower temperature or a little farther away from the heat source to allow the interior to cook completely while the outside browns. Marinating and basting also help keep leaner meats moist.

Do not season meats until just before cooking, as the salt can draw out the juices.

Preheat the broiler or prepare an outdoor charcoal fire. Line the broiler rack with foil for easier cleaning. Trim as much fat as possible from the meat and remove any visible connective tissue. If the meat has been marinating, drain off excess liquid.

① Arrange the meat on the lined rack, brush with a little oil, and season with salt and pepper.

② The broiler rack should be about 3–4 inches from the heat; if barbecuing, keep the rack about 4–6 inches from the heat. Cook 3–4 minutes until well-browned, then using tongs, turn the meat and cook to the desired degree of doneness. Serve with flavored butter.

FOR THICK CUTS
For Chateaubriand or butterflied leg of lamb, lower the broiler heat or move the barbecue grill to a higher position over the coals to finish cooking, once the exterior is browned. Alternatively, after browning, transfer the meat to a preheated oven to complete cooking evenly.

STIR-FRYING

Stir-frying is based on Chinese wok cooking. The wok is a large, rounded pan which allows foods to be stirred and tossed for quick, even cooking. A special shovel-like spatula, wooden spoon, or chopsticks are used for stirring.

All ingredients must be prepared ahead of time. Meat and vegetables should be cut into small cubes or strips of equal size, and any aromatics or sauce ingredients prepared.

❶ Slice the meat into thin strips or small cubes. Marinate briefly in a Chinese-style marinade, if desired.

❷ Heat the dry wok or skillet over medium-high heat until very hot. Pour in the oil and swirl to coat the wok completely.

❸ When the oil is very hot but not smoking, add the recipe ingredients in batches, as directed. Do not overcrowd or the food will steam, rather than fry. You may need to remove one ingredient and set aside while cooking another.

❹ When all the ingredients are cooked, pour in the sauce or liquid as the recipe directs. It will bubble and begin to thicken. Return any ingredients removed earlier and stir until well-coated; serve.

Moist-heat Methods

Moist-heat cooking uses moisture as well as heat to cook meat. Slow simmering for a long period tenderizes tougher cuts of meat and brings out rich flavors. The cooking liquid is then generally used to make a sauce or gravy, such as with a pot roast or brisket. However, if the meats are salted or cured, like ham or corned beef, the liquid should not be salted or used for sauce. Cooking in liquid often helps to draw some of the saltiness out of the meat. Meats subjected to moist heat are cooked to well done. Test by piercing with a fork; it should pull apart easily – hence the expression *fork-tender*. Undercooked, the meat will be tough and chewy; overcooked, the meat will fall apart or have a stringy texture.

BRAISING

Braised meats are first browned, then cooked in a liquid which will form the base of a sauce. Although tender cuts can be used, the technique is best suited to tougher cuts with more connective tissue which makes a rich gravy. The long, slow-moist cooking helps tenderize the meat. Smaller cuts of meat can be lightly floured, which seals the meat and helps thicken the gravy, or the gravy can be thickened at the end of the cooking, if you like. Braises can be cooked on top of the stove or transferred to the oven for more even cooking. The latter method helps prevent scorching and leaves the top of the stove free for other cooking.

❶ Over medium-high heat, heat the oil in a large, heavy Dutch oven or casserole with a tight-fitting lid. Add the meat and brown well on all sides, turning as necessary. Remove to a plate. Add any onions or other vegetables to the casserole, stirring to color. Pour in any other liquids, such as tomato sauce or wine, and any herbs or seasonings. Stir well to combine.

❷ Return the meat to the Dutch oven, cover tightly, and bring to a boil. Reduce heat to low and simmer 1½–2 hours, depending on the size of the meat. Alternatively, transfer the Dutch oven to a preheated 325°F oven for 1½–2 hours, basting occasionally. Place the meat on a cutting board, strain and degrease the sauce, season, and thicken. Slice the meat crosswise into slices and serve with the gravy.

The procedure for stewing is very similar to braising, although stews are usually made with bite-sized or small pieces of meat. Stews can be *brown* or *white*. Brown stews involve browning the meat pieces before cooking in liquid. White stews include *fricasses*, which lightly sears the meat in fat without actually coloring, before adding liquid, and *blanquettes*, which blanch the meat before cooking in liquid. Both dishes are white or creamy in color.

Stews use many of the same cuts as braises, which should be well-trimmed. Using a good full-bodied stock is the key to a rich flavorful stew. Red meats such as beef, lamb, or game are generally used for brown stews while pale meats like veal, pork, and chicken appear in fricasses and blanquettes. From the famous *Boeuf Bourguinon* to Morrocan *tagines*, almost every cuisine has a classic stew recipe.

INGREDIENTS

¼ lb/4 oz thick-cut bacon or
    lean salt pork, diced
3½ lbs lean stewing beef,
    preferably chuck or shin, cut
    into 2-in pieces
1 onion, chopped
1 carrot, chopped
3 tablespoons all-purpose flour
3 cups/1½ pints full-bodied dry
    red wine
2 tablespoons tomato paste
large bouquet garni (p.8)
3 cups/1½ pints rich beef stock
salt and pepper
2 tablespoons butter
¾ lb/12 oz pearl onions
¾ lb/12 oz button mushrooms,
    halved if large
2 tablespoons chopped fresh
    parsley

1 Put the bacon or salt pork in a large, heavy-based Dutch oven or casserole and set over medium-high heat. As the bacon or salt pork begins to splutter, stir occasionally. Cook until crisp and golden, then use a slotted spoon to place on a plate. Spoon off all but 2 tablespoons of the fat.

2 Add enough meat to fit in one layer and brown on all sides until well colored; you will need to work in batches. Transfer each batch to a plate until all the meat is well browned. Pour off all but 2 tablespoons of the remaining fat.

3 Add the chopped onion, carrot, and garlic. Cook 3–4 minutes, until softened and colored, stirring frequently. Sprinkle the flour over and stir constantly.

4 Gradually pour in the wine, tomato paste, and stock; season with salt and pepper. Add the bouquet garni and tie to the casserole handle. Bring vegetables and stock to a boil, scraping up the brown bits from the base of the pan.

5 Return meat to the Dutch oven. Add a little more stock, if necessary, to cover the ingredients. Cover tightly and simmer gently over low heat for about 3 hours until the meat is tender.

6 About ½ hour before the end of the cooking time, heat the butter in a skillet over medium-high heat. Add the pearl onions and fry, stirring frequently until golden. Remove to a plate. Add the mushrooms to the pan and sauté until golden, 3–4 minutes, stirring frequently. Add the reserved onions and the mushrooms to the stew, pushing them into the gravy.

7 Cook until the meat and vegetables are tender. Remove and discard the bouquet garni, stir in the parsley, and serve.

Vegetables

Though the vegetarian path is still the choice of a minority, its influence has permeated far beyond. No longer are vegetables boiled to a pulp, their vitamins lost to the water. Now the guideline is: the less cooked, the better – raw is often best. Techniques like stir-frying, steaming, and roasting keep in both flavor and goodness; careful preparation too is invaluable in preserving vegetable virtues.

Roots and Tubers

Roots and tubers grow underground and include potatoes, sweet potatoes and yams, carrots, turnips, parsnips, celeriac (celery root), beet, Jerusalem artichokes (sunchokes), rutabaga, Kohlrabi (technically a cabbage), salsify, and scorzonera. Red and white radishes, long radishes, and daikon (mooli) are also root vegetables.

Most root vegetables store well in a cool, dark place, and many can be interchanged. Most need to be cooked until just tender, and the general rule is to start cooking in cold water, bring to a boil, and simmer until tender to avoid breaking up. Roots and tubers are extremely versatile and can be cooked in many ways: steamed, boiled and mashed, roasted, sautéed, baked, fried, or gratinéed. Their high water content makes them ideal for microwaving. Most roots and tubers need to be peeled before cooking, although young potatoes and carrots can be trimmed and scrubbed.

PEELERS

There are different kinds of peelers available. Choose a style you feel comfortable with or which is suitable to the size and shape of the vegetable, such as a wide blade for larger vegetables like potatoes, or a fixed or swivel blade for carrots or parsnips. A sharp knife is best for thicker-skinned celeriacs.

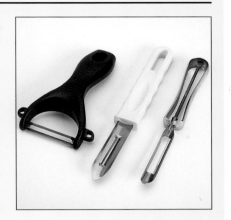

CARROTS AND PARSNIPS

Probably the sweetest of the root vegetables, carrots and parsnips are prepared in the same way. Although they can be eaten raw, parsnips are generally cooked.

PREPARING
To prepare carrots or parsnips, trim the ends, then peel. If preparing parsnips ahead, drop into acidulated water to prevent darkening. Carrots and parsnips can be sliced into rounds, cut lengthwise for roasting, cut into batons or julienne strips for stir-frying or salads, or chopped.

COOKING
To cook, drop into boiling salted water and simmer until tender, about 5–6 minutes for sliced carrots or parsnips; 7–9 minutes for whole baby carrots, or, cook 1 pound carrots, sliced, in a deep skillet with ¼ cup/2 oz water or stock, 1 tablespoon butter, and 1 tablespoon sugar or honey, tightly covered, until just tender, about 5 minutes. Uncover and allow excess liquid to evaporate until carrots are lightly glazed and tender.

BLANCHING
To blanch parsnips for pan-frying or roasting, cover with cold water, bring to a boil, and simmer 1 minute; drain. Fry in butter until tender and golden, 8–10 minutes. To purée or mash, cook until very tender, then mash or purée.

ROASTING
To roast parsnips, heat about ¼ cup/2 oz oil and 1 tablespoon butter in a roasting pan. Add the blanched, drained parsnips and roast until crisp and tender, 35–40 minutes in a preheated oven at 400°F, turning occasionally.

STIR-FRY
To stir-fry carrots or parsnips, heat 1 tablespoon vegetable oil in a wok or skillet over high heat. Add 1 teaspoon of sesame oil and up to 1 pound vegetables cut into julienne strips. Stir-fry until just tender, 2–3 minutes.

TURNIPS, KOHLRABI, AND RUTABAGA (SWEDE)

Turnip has a slightly peppery flavor, which makes it ideal for glazing or steaming. Kohlrabi has a similar flavor. Rutabaga is often confused with turnip, but is slightly blander and has a yellow color – it requires a slightly longer cooking time.

TURNIPS
To prepare turnips, trim the ends and peel with a vegetable peeler. The skin of the rutabaga is thicker, so a sharp knife will be necessary to remove the thick skin and roots. Slice, cube, or chop as recipe directs.

KOHLRABI
To prepare kohlrabi, cut off the root end, then cut off the leaves (they can be cooked like spinach). Peel, slice, and cook as for turnips. Can also be sliced raw and used in salads.

COOKING
To cook, drop into boiling salted water and simmer until tender (9–12 minutes), or steam over boiling water for 8–12 minutes, or, braise in a deep skillet with a teaspoon of butter and about ¼ cup/2 oz water or stock until tender, 4–6 minutes.

CELERIAC (CELERY ROOT)

This relative of the celery stalk is sweet and delicate, but peppery. It is ideal boiled and mashed or cut into julienne sticks and served raw with mustard mayonnaise.

PREPARATION
To prepare, use a chef's knife to peel off the thick, knobbly skin and roots. If using raw for salads, drop into acidulated water as celeriac discolors when exposed to light and air. Cut into cubes, slices, julienne strips, or as recipe directs.

COOKING
To cook, cover about 1 pound cubed celeriac and 1 medium diced potato with cold water. Bring to a boil over medium-high heat, reduce heat and simmer until very tender, 10–15 minutes. Drain, return to pan, and mash with 1 tablespoon butter and a little milk or cream.

PUREEING
Use a potato dicer or food mill to purée tender chunks of celeriac, swede, or parsnip. Season with a little butter, salt, pepper, and nutmeg or a dusting of Parmesan cheese.

HEATING OIL FOR DEEP FRYING

Heat at least 3 inches of vegetable oil in a saucepan or deep fryer over medium-high heat until it reaches 375°F on a deep fat thermometer. If you do not have a deep fat thermometer, toss a cube of bread into the hot oil; it should sizzle and turn deep golden brown in about 60 seconds. Do not add too much food to the oil at once; this will lower the temperature of the oil and produce oily or soggy food.

For the best results, French fries are cooked twice, once at a lower temperature (360°F) to make them tender, then a second time at a slightly higher temperature (375°F) to crisp and color them.

POTATOES

This vegetable can be cooked in so many ways it is not possible to count them. Potatoes can be "old" or "new," waxy or floury, white or red-skinned. Choose a low starch, waxy type for boiling, steaming, sautéeing, or using cold in salads, as they keep their shape. For baking, mashing, or using in gratins, choose a floury, starchy potato with a light fluffy texture; both types can be fried. Sweet potatoes, white, yellow, or orange-fleshed, are best boiled, baked, or mashed. Yams, another tuber, can be used like sweet potatoes, but are slightly less sweet. Do not refrigerate potatoes as low temperatures cause the flesh to blacken. Potatoes turn green and become toxic if exposed to bright light, so store them in a cool, dark place. Potatoes discolor when exposed to air, so if preparing ahead, peel and drop into a bowl of cold water for up to 2 hours.

SAUTÉEING
To sauté or fry, heat enough oil to cover the bottom of a heavy-based skillet over medium heat until very hot. Add the potatoes (raw or precooked) and allow them to color on one side before turning. Continue to cook until crisp and golden and tender, about 10–12 minutes.

PREPARING
To prepare, scrub the skins if baking. To prevent the thin skin on new potatoes from splitting, peel a strip of skin from around the center. Otherwise, peel potatoes with a vegetable peeler. Slice, cube, dice or prepare as recipe directs. Boil, steam, or mash as for rutabaga (p.74).

DEEP-FRY
❶ To deep-fry French fries, cut peeled potatoes into batons or sticks about ¼ inch thick. Soak in cold water for ½ hour, drain well, and dry in a clean towel.

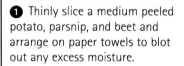

BAKING
To bake white or sweet potatoes, pierce each potato with a skewer or knife point in several places to prevent the potato from bursting. Arrange on a foil-lined baking sheet or directly on the oven shelf and bake in a 400°F oven until tender, about 1¼ hours.

❷ Heat the oil (see box, page 74) and fry the potatoes in small batches until just tender and lightly golden, 4–6 minutes depending on their size. Remove with slotted spoon or in fryer basket and drain on paper towels.

❸ When all the potatoes have been cooked, fry them a second time at a slightly higher temperature until crisp and brown, about 2 minutes. Drain on paper towels, sprinkle with salt, and serve hot.

ROOT VEGETABLE CHIPS

These homemade root vegetable chips make a delicious alternative to purchased potato chips.

❶ Thinly slice a medium peeled potato, parsnip, and beet and arrange on paper towels to blot out any excess moisture.

❷ Heat at least 3 inches vegetable oil in a saucepan or deep fryer to 375°F (see box, page 74). Fry the vegetable slices in batches until crisp and golden, about 3 minutes, shaking the basket or stirring. Drain on paper towels.

❸ Arrange on a plate and sprinkle with salt. Serve with cocktails or as a snack.

BEETS

Popular in central and eastern European cuisines, beets contain a crimson dye called betanin, which bleeds into other foods and can be quite stunning.

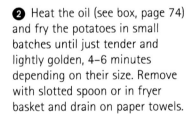

Wash with a soft brush, but do not pierce the skin. Although beets can be boiled or steamed, they are most easily cooked in the microwave. Arrange 3–4 medium beets in a microwave-safe dish. Cover tightly with plastic wrap and microwave on High (full power) 8–10 minutes. Allow to stand 4–5 minutes. Or, wrap in foil and oven bake until tender, about 1 hour in a 400°F oven. Cool, then slip off skins (wear rubber gloves to prevent dye from staining your fingers.)

Pods, Seeds, and Corn

This group of vegetables are the seeds of their plant; sometimes only the seed is eaten (like peas), other times, the whole pod is eaten (snowpeas). Although corn is technically a grain, the kernels we eat are actually the plant seeds. These vegetables are generally high in protein and carbohydrates.

Beans and peas are members of the legume family, vegetables with double-seamed pods containing a single row of seeds; this group contains a huge variety of green beans from around the world. In spite of regional differences, most of them are prepared and cooked in similar ways. Young varieties of edible pods like snowpeas are eaten in the pod while the seed is immature; shelled peas and beans like garden peas and fresh fava beans are removed from the pod to eat fresh. Others are left to dry (see Grains and Legumes, page 86).

Green vegetables, unlike root vegetables, are best cooked quickly by dropping into boiling salted water and boiling rapidly for 2–10 minutes until just tender, but still crisp and crunchy with a bright color.

FRESH BEANS

Used for their edible pods, this group of immature beans includes green beans, string beans, snap beans, yellow wax beans, and Chinese long beans. Trim the ends, pulling off any strings by "snapping" the stem ends and pulling the strings which may still be attached along the sides (although many new varieties are stringless). For young, tender beans, trim with kitchen scissors or a knife. Edible pea pods such as snowpeas and the deliciously sweet sugar-snap peas are prepared the same way.

All fresh beans can be eaten raw, lightly blanched, steamed, sautéed, stir-fried, or microwaved – they are best lightly cooked.

To prepare snap beans or flat beans, cut diagonally into 1-inch pieces.

Long beans or flat beans are sometimes cut vertically into long slivers; beans cut this way will cook more quickly.

SHELLING PEAS AND BEANS

Fresh shelling peas and beans have a short season and unfortunately begin to lose their flavor and sweetness soon after picking, which is why they are most widely available frozen and canned. The frozen varieties are of very good quality, often quick frozen within hours after picking. Fresh garden peas, fava beans, or lima beans, need only light steaming or blanching until tender, 3–5 minutes.

SHELLING PEAS
Press the pod between your thumb and finger to open, then push the peas out. Rinse well before using (discard the pods).

SKINNING FAVA BEANS
Make a small slit in the skin with a sharp knife and squeeze each bean between your thumb and finger; the bean will pop out easily. For more mature beans, blanch in boiling water 30–60 seconds, refresh, and proceed as above.

OKRA

Okra is an unusual, five-sided, elongated pod, sometimes called ladyfingers. Brought to the New World by African slaves and French settlers, it is now used in Creole, Cajun, Southern, and Caribbean cooking. When okra is cooked for long periods of time, it develops a gelatinous texture used to thicken gumbos and stews. Choose small to medium pods with no soft spots. Okra can be boiled, stewed, pickled, or deep-fried.

To prepare okra, do not wash until ready to cook. Using a small sharp knife, trim the stem evenly; avoid piercing it. Cook in stainless steel or other non-corrosive cookware to avoid discoloration.

CORN

Although corn is a grain, its kernels, like peas, are seeds. Like peas, corn contains sugars which begin turning to starch as soon as it is picked, so the fresher the corn, the better and sweeter. Traditionally boiled on the cob and served with butter, corn can be broiled or grilled on the barbecue in or out of the husk; or the kernels can be removed from the cob and braised in cream until tender, or used as a base for chowders. Cooked corn kernels can be added to salads or stir-fried with rice dishes, or used in fritters and soups. Choose ears of corn with small pale kernels in even rows with pale silks.

To husk corn, pull off the outer husks and silks; break or cut the stem if necessary. Use a small vegetable brush to remove any excess silks. Cook whole ears of corn in boiling water with 1 teaspoon sugar until tender, about 5 minutes.

Fruit Vegetables

Botanically speaking, tomatoes, eggplants, sweet bell peppers, and avocados are fruits, but are usually treated like vegetables in the kitchen. They each require different preparation and cooking techniques. Although each can be used as a principal ingredient, they can also be used as background or flavoring for other dishes.

Vine-ripened tomatoes have an intense perfume and superior flavor and texture – unfortunately, they are extremely fragile and do not travel well. They are only available during the summer and early fall. Greenhouse and hydroponic tomatoes (grown in water without soil) often look good but lack flavor, but they are available year round. Look for tomatoes grown for flavor.

There are many varieties of tomato available, ranging from the giant American "beefsteak" tomato to the thumbnail-sized cherry tomatoes so popular in salads. Tomatoes can be round or long and range in color from red or yellow to green.

PREPARING TOMATOES

Many recipes call for peeled, seeded, and chopped tomatoes; this preparation is called *concasée* in French. It may seem complicated, but the result is worth it, providing a fresh intense tomato flavor with no skins or seeds.

Core the tomatoes, then, using a small sharp knife, score the bottom of each tomato making an X just penetrating the skins. Drop the tomatoes into rapidly boiling water for 10–20 seconds, depending on their ripeness. Remove and refresh in ice water.

Remove the tomatoes from the water and peel off the skin, which will have begun to roll back.

Quarter each tomato and, using a small sharp knife, scrape out the seeds, or cut each tomato crosswise in half and squeeze out the seeds, using the knife to scrape out any remaining seeds. Slice or chop as recipe directs.

FRESH TOMATO SAUCE

INGREDIENTS
1–2 tablespoons olive oil
1 onion, finely chopped
1–2 cloves garlic, finely chopped
1 lb vine-ripened or plum
    tomatoes, peeled, seeded, and
    chopped
½ teaspoon dried thyme
1 teaspoon sugar (optional)
1 tablespoon tomato paste
¼ cup/2 oz water
2 tablespoons fresh chopped or
    torn basil leaves
salt and pepper

❶ Heat the oil in a large skillet over medium heat. Add the onion and cook until soft and translucent, 5–8 minutes, stirring occasionally. Add the garlic and cook for 2 more minutes, until fragrant.

❷ Add the tomatoes, dried thyme, sugar (if using), and tomato paste and water. Bring to a boil, then lower the heat and simmer for 25–30 minutes, stirring occasionally, to a purée-like consistency. Stir in the basil and season. Cook 5 more minutes until flavors blend.

BROILING OR BARBECUING EGGPLANT

These large, plump, pear-shaped fruit vegetables, with shiny purple-black skins, are related to tomatoes. There are small round or elongated varieties available called Asian or Chinese eggplant. Both varieties have a pale greenish-gray bland flesh which absorbs flavors during cooking; they can be used interchangably.

Eggplant can be sliced crosswise or lengthwise, cubed or diced. It can be fried in oil (coated or uncoated) until tender, about 5 minutes, or braised in oil and 3–4 tablespoons stock or water until tender, about 10 minutes.

❶ To prepare the eggplant, cut in half lengthwise. Using the tip of a sharp knife, score the surface of the flesh.

❷ To cook, set the eggplant halves on a wire rack on a foil-lined broiler pan and brush each cut surface with a little oil. Broil at least 4 inches from the heat until tender and colored, 12–15 minutes. (Slices can be cooked in the same way, broil 8–10 minutes or as recipe directs.)

PEPPERS

Sweet peppers are members of the *capsicum* family. They can be red, yellow, green, black, purple, or orange. Pimientoes are red peppers cultivated for roasting or canning: they are sweet with a bright reddish-orange color. Sweet peppers add color and flavor to many dishes, as well as making a delicious vegetable. Green peppers have a slightly grassy-bitter taste; yellow and red are the ripest and sweetest. Peppers can be cored and diced or sliced for salads and crudités, or fried, sautéed, broiled, or stuffed and baked.

PREPARING PEPPERS
If the pepper is to be left whole for stuffing, cut off the stem end and scoop out the seeds with a spoon. Cut a very thin slice off the bottom end to allow the pepper to stand without wobbling. Prepare as the recipe directs. If the pepper is to be sliced or chopped, the flesh can be removed more easily.

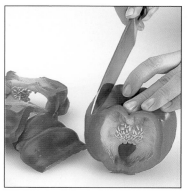

Trim the stem and bottom ends of the pepper, then cut off the 4 sides or "cheeks" from the center cavity, trim any remaining white ribs. You will have 4 "square" sides to slice or chop. Cut as recipe directs.

Alternatively, trim the stem and bottom ends off the pepper. Cut the pepper "circle" lengthwise and open it out to a flat strip. Remove the core, ribs and seeds. Cut into strips or as recipe directs.

ROASTING PEPPERS

Roasted or broiled peppers have an intensely sweet yet mildly smoky flavor. Garnished with a little virgin olive oil, balsamic vinegar, black pepper, and basil, they are delicious with meat or as a vegetable.

1 Arrange peppers on a rack on a foil-lined broiler pan. Broil close to the heat, turning frequently until all sides are slightly charred and blistered. Put the peppers in a plastic bag and seal, or cover with a bowl; the steam trapped inside the bag or bowl helps loosen the skin.

2 When the peppers are cool enough to handle, peel off the charred skin, using a small sharp knife if necessary. Cut out the stem and core, scraping out any seeds; leave whole, halve, or slice.

Gourds and Squashes

Squashes are a member of the gourd or *Cucurbitaceae* family, which contains hundreds of varieties around the world. Gourds tend to be found in warm regions such as Africa and India, but most squashes are native to the Americas. There are many varieties in a huge range of colors, shapes, and sizes, but for the cook they can be divided into summer squash and winter squash.

PREPARING SUMMER SQUASH

Summer squash, characterized by the zucchini, is soft-skinned with a mild tender flesh, which can be eaten raw or lightly cooked by boiling, steaming, or stir-frying. Larger varieties can be hollowed out for stuffing and baking. A Mediterranean specialty, the flowers of zucchini or summer squash can be stuffed and deep-fried. Chayote, a summer squash used extensively in Central America and the Pacific, has a large central seed. It is bland and needs a slightly longer cooking time than other summer squashes. There are also the pretty, scalloped-edge patty-pan squash, the yellow or green crookneck, the straightneck squash, and the yellow zucchini. Some of these are now grown as miniature varieties.

Picked when immature, thin-skinned summer squash does not need to be peeled, but should be washed to remove any sand or grit.

Trim the ends, then slice or chop as the recipe directs. Fry in butter or oil over medium-high heat until tender, about 5 minutes.

To make a zucchini boat for stuffing, trim the stem end and cut in half lengthwise. Using a small sharp knife, score a ¼-inch border around the edge. Use a spoon to scoop out the seeds and flesh. Fill as recipe directs.

1 To prepare patty-pan squash, leave whole and trim ends, or trim and cut into halves or quarters.

2 To cook, steam over boiling water until just tender, 4–6 minutes. Alternatively stir-fry in butter or oil 2–4 minutes until tender-crisp and golden.

PREPARING WINTER SQUASH

Winter squash are picked when fully matured and so have thick hard skins with firm, compact, often darker-colored, more flavorful flesh. After removing the large seeds, the flesh can be removed from the shell before or after cooking, but should not be eaten raw. It can be roasted, baked, steamed, sautéed, or microwaved. It is ideal for puréeing and making soups or sweet pies such as pumpkin pie.

To prepare acorn, butternut, or hubbard squash, cut in half. Then using a large spoon, scrape out seeds and fibers from the center cavity of each half.

To remove the flesh before cooking, use a chef's knife to peel off the thick skin. To cook winter squash cubes, drop into boiling salted water and cook until tender, 8–10 minutes.

To purée winter squash, cook in boiling water until very tender 12–15 minutes. Drain well, then mash or process in a food processor or until smooth. Add 2 tablespoons butter (or milk or cream) and a little nutmeg.

To bake winter squash, place squash halves cut side down and bake in a preheated 180°C (350°F/Gas 7) oven for 25 minutes. Turn cut side up, dot with butter, sprinkle with a little cinnamon, and drizzle on some maple syrup. Bake, covered with foil, 20 minutes longer. Uncover and bake 5–10 minutes more until tender and lightly colored.

CUCUMBERS

Cucumbers, members of the gourd family, can be divided into two types, slicing and pickling. Although there are many varieties, the common green slicing cucumber is the one more often seen in supermarkets. This cucumber generally has a waxy coating which should be peeled before eating. The European hothouse cucumber is generally longer and thinner and has a thinner skin, so it is not necessary to peel it. It also has fewer seeds. The cool, refreshing taste and crunchy texture of cucumber makes it ideal in salads, in Middle Eastern dips such as *tzatziki,* and in Indian relishes or *raitas.*

CUCUMBER GARNISHES
Use a canalle knife to make deep lengthwise ridges or use a vegetable peeler to remove alternate lengthwise strips from the whole cucumber. Cut crosswise in thin slices.

Cut each thin slice from the center to the edge. Twist cut edges in the opposite direction and stand on their side.

DICING
Peel if recipe directs or if you like. Quarter the cucumber lengthwise, then cut off the core triangle of seeds from each quarter. Cut into long strips, then into 2-inch batons, or dice or chop.

BUSY COOKS

To microwave winter squash, cut into cubes and arrange in a microwave-safe dish. Dot with butter, add 1 tablespoon water to the dish, and cover tightly with plastic wrap. Microwave on High (full power) 5–8 minutes, depending on the amount, until tender.

Greens and Salad Greens

Greens refer to a wide variety of leafy green vegetables, some of which can be eaten raw, but are often cooked. Greens are eaten in most countries around the world. Some greens like mustard greens, sorrel, spinach, Swiss chard, dandelion, arugula, watercress, and turnip greens have a strong peppery flavor. Other greens like lettuces and salad greens are blander and are almost always eaten raw. Greens can be roughly divided into 2 categories: hearty greens (most often cooked) and salad greens (most often eaten raw), although the divisions are often blurred. All greens have a very high water content and shrink drastically when cooked; allow about half a pound per person if the greens are cooked.

HEARTY GREENS

Many of these sturdy, leafy greens (sometimes called pot herbs) can be eaten raw in salads when they are young and tender, but they are rarely found at this stage. Most are older and tougher, and need cooking to tenderize them and soften their often robust flavor.

SALAD GREENS

The major salad green, lettuce, can be divided into crisphead and butterhead, or soft-leaf, salads. Trim off the roots and wash well. Always dress salads gently at the last minute, so the dressing does not wilt the leaves.

PREPARING GREENS

Wash all greens well to remove any sand and grit. Immerse in a sink or bowl of cold water and soak 3–4 minutes, swishing the leaves around. Gently lift out of the water into a colander or strainer to drain. Repeat several times until no sand or grit remains on the bottom of the sink or bowl. Drain, shake well, and pile leaves in a colander.

Remove any large, tough stalks from spinach, kale, or other greens by gripping the leaf with one hand and pulling the stalk up and away from the leaf.

Separate the leaves from the stalks of Swiss chard by cutting the stalk out in a long V shape.

COOKING GREENS

Some greens like spinach take only seconds, while others benefit from longer braising or tenderizing.

To cook spinach, put the leaves in a saucepan with just the water which clings to the leaves from washing. Set over medium heat and cook gently until just wilted, 2–3 minutes, or stir-fry in a little butter or oil until wilted, 1–2 minutes. To blanch, dip into boiling water for 30 seconds.

If using cooked spinach or other greens in another preparation such as creamed spinach or a braised dish, turn into a strainer and press out as much liquid as possible with a wooden spoon. Use leaves whole or chop as recipe directs.

Stir-fry bok choy or Swiss chard in a little butter or oil until just wilted and tender, 2–6 minutes. For an oriental flavor, season with a little soy sauce and a drop or two of sesame oil.

Cut the stalk into 1-inch pieces and tear or shred the leaves; cook each separately as the leaves cook more quickly than the stalks. The leaf and stalk of young tender bok choy may be left together as the cooking time is very short. Separate from the root and trim if they are still attached.

To shred bok choy or chard leaves, stack the leaves and roll together, then slice crosswise into thick or thin shreds as the recipe directs.

Cabbage and Brassicas

Cabbage, a member of the *Brassica* family, is one of the oldest vegetables cultivated by man. There are many kinds of cabbage, mostly characterized by round heads of compact leaves, though some are flattened, elongated, or more loosely packed. Cabbage is generally a cold-weather vegetable, inexpensive, widely available, and easy to prepare and cook, which may explain its wide use in many cultures. It can be eaten raw as in coleslaw, pickled as in sauerkraut, or cooked in a wide variety of ways. Do not overcook cabbage, as it becomes soggy and has a very unpleasant smell. Look for cabbages heavy for their size, discarding any tough outer leaves.

White cabbage, sometimes called round or Dutch cabbage, is the most common. Usually trimmed of its darker, tough outer leaves, it has a firm, pale green head and solid core with a robust flavor. It can be shredded for crisp salads or coleslaw, stir-fried, braised, boiled, simmered in soups, or stuffed. This is the cabbage used for sauerkraut. Savory cabbage or curly cabbage has slightly looser leaves and a purple tinge, and is more delicate in flavor.

Red cabbage has a brilliant purple color and a slightly sweeter taste. It needs a slightly longer cooking time than white cabbage and is often braised with onion and apple to accompany duck or game. An acid such as vinegar is usually added to set the color. For this reason a little vinegar is added to braised cabbage as well as the apple. A little sugar usually complements the acid, giving it a sweet and sour flavor.

Chinese cabbage, sometimes called Napa cabbage, has pale greenish-yellow elongated leaves. It is milder in flavor than white cabbage, can be eaten raw or cooked, and is an ingredient in many Chinese stir-fries.

BRUSSELS SPROUTS

These miniature cabbages originated in Belgium where they are grown on thick stalks. Rarely eaten raw, they have a strong, nutty flavor which goes well with game, duck, and other rich meats. They are sometimes braised with chestnuts, and in Britain are a traditional accompaniment to the Christmas turkey. Boil or steam until just tender, 7–10 minutes. .

❶ To prepare Brussels sprouts, remove any loose or slightly yellow outer leaves.

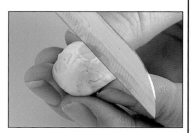

❷ With a sharp knife, score an X in the base for more even cooking

PREPARING CABBAGE

To prepare cabbage, cut in half and cut out the core in a V shape. If whole leaves are needed for stuffing, pull them apart, detaching them intact from the stem, then blanch as for spinach leaves, increasing the time slightly; refresh in cold water.

To shred, set one half cut side down, and cut crosswise into thick or thin slices as the recipe directs.

BROCCOLI AND CAULIFLOWER

Members of the cabbage family, broccoli and cauliflower both have tightly grouped flower buds coming from a single stalk. They can be eaten raw in salads and crudité platters or cooked in a variety of ways, whole or separated into flowerets. Boil or steam cauliflowerets until tender, 5–10 minutes.

CAULIFLOWER
To prepare cauliflower, remove the outer green leaves and the core from the stem end. Break the cauliflower into pieces, then break off flowerets.

BROCCOLI
To prepare broccoli, trim the thick woody stem and break off small flowerets. Alternatively, leave the stalk longer but trim it. Split the head of broccoli into quarters and trim the tough outer skin from the outside of the base.

Mushrooms and Truffles

Mushrooms, members of the *fungi* family, are one of the oldest foods eaten by man. There are many different varieties which vary in size, shape, color, and flavor, but all have a central stalk with an umbrella-shaped cap.

There are two types of mushroom, cultivated and wild, and most of them are prepared and cooked in similar ways. The cultivated mushroom, or common white mushroom, has been successfully produced since the late 1800's. Very young white closed-cap mushrooms are called button mushrooms. They are mild in flavor and widely available year round. Flat mushrooms, sometimes called field mushrooms or portabellas, are ideal for broiling. A growing number of previously wild varieties are now being cultivated. Mushrooms like the shitake, enokitake (enoki or pinhead), cloud ears, and oyster are all now widely available.

Wild mushrooms are found all over the world, most frequently in late summer and fall, in many woods and fields providing the perfect conditions. The flavor is intensely earthy, and they should always be cooked before eating. *Many mushrooms can be dangerous, so do not pick or gather wild mushrooms unless you are accompanied by an expert mycologist or guide, and always purchase wild mushrooms from a reputable dealer.* Wild mushrooms such as morels, boletus, also called cepe or porcini, parasols, wood hedgehogs, blewits, chanterelles, horn of plenty, and chicken of the wood are all expensive, but so highly flavored that a little goes a long way. Some of the wild varieties are available dried: morels, boletus (cepe or porcini), shitake, matsutake, and cloud ear can all be purchased dried and are easily reconstituted. The most famous fungi is the truffle. This pungent, black treasure is really a tuber, sniffed out of the oak forests of the French Perigord (black) and Italian Piedmont (white) by pigs or dogs. The fresh variety is prohibitively expensive, but they are available in jars, and although they lose much of their aroma, even a small amount can add intense flavor to foods.

Wrap fresh mushrooms loosely in paper towels and refrigerate up to 3 days. Do not store in plastic bags as the moisture will cause rapid deterioration.

PREPARING MUSHROOMS

Cultivated mushrooms should not be washed before using. Use a mushroom brush or soft toothbrush to brush off any earth or grit, or wipe with a damp paper towel. If they are very earthy or sandy, plunge quickly into a bowl of cold water, lift out and drain; dry immediately. Trim the stalks.

Wild mushrooms are often very sandy and do need washing. Plunge into several changes of cold water, lift out, and drain. Trim off any woody stems and tough outer edges. Morels sometimes need soaking to draw out the sand.

To prepare mushrooms, clean them and trim the stems. Quarter large mushrooms or slice as recipe directs. Use a stainless steel knife as other materials can discolor mushrooms. Sprinkle with a little lemon juice to prevent darkening if preparing ahead or chopping a large quantity.

COOKING MUSHROOMS

Heat butter or oil in a skillet over medium-high heat until very hot, but not smoking. Add the mushrooms, and sauté or stir-fry 3–4 minutes until golden and tender. Continue cooking until any liquid evaporates.

Open-cap or field mushrooms can be brushed with butter or oil and broiled 4 inches from the heat until browned and tender, 6–8 minutes. Baste occasionally.

The Onion Family

These strong flavored, aromatic vegetables are members of the lily family. Onions, scallions, leeks, shallots, and garlic are sometimes used as vegetables, but are most often used as flavorings in other dishes. Chives are the only true herb in the onion family. Onions vary in color, size, texture, and flavor and are used in every cuisine around the world.

Onions and their relatives can be used raw or cooked. Their flavor varies from mild and sweet to pungently strong. Generally, the milder the climate of origin, the sweeter the onion. Large mild varieties of the stronger common yellow onion, or globe onion, are named after their place of origin: the Spanish Valencia, Hawaiian Maui, the Bermuda, the Vidalia and the Walla Walla from the southern states. These sweet onions are best sliced raw in salads or on sandwiches and hamburgers. They are also excellent for stuffing or grilling on the barbecue. Large white onions are slightly milder than yellow ones. Red onions are sweet and best eaten raw.

Pearl onions, sometimes called pickling onions or silverskins, are harvested when they are about 1 inch in diameter. Boiling onions are slightly larger, and cocktail onions are tiny white onions kept small by compact planting, which inhibits their growth. Baby onions are available peeled and frozen, and are often used in stews and braised meat dishes. Long scallions or green onions are immature yellow onions grown for their milder flavor. Leeks are the mildest and sweetest of the onion family, frequently used to flavor soups and stocks.

PREPARING ONIONS

Use a small sharp knife to cut the stem end and peel off the papery skin; leave the root end intact to help hold the onion together. Trim the root ends of scallions and remove wilting leaves.

❶ Cut the onion in half lengthwise. Set each half cut side down on a cutting board. With a sharp knife make a series of vertical cuts, cutting just to, but not through, the root. Then make a series of horizontal cuts from the stem in toward the root.

❷ Cut the onions crosswise, allowing it to fall into dice. If you want a finer dice, continue chopping the onion, using a rocking motion with the knife against the board.

ONION RINGS
To cut onion rings, steady the peeled onion against the board and cut crosswise into thick or thin slices. Alternatively, halve the onion, set it cut side down, and cut crosswise into half rings.

PREPARING LEEKS

Leeks are famous for hiding sand and grit between their leaves and need vigorous washing.

Discard any tough or yellow outer leaves and trim the root end. Trim some of the green top, as the recipe directs, and, unless using whole, slit the leek in half or quarters from the top into the white part. Plunge leeks into cold water down to the root, shaking to loosen any grit. Repeat if necessary. Slice, chop, or julienne as recipe directs. If using whole, do not slit; soak in cold water, shaking to remove any grit.

COOKING ONIONS AND LEEKS

Onions should be cooked slowly in butter or oil until soft and transparent. This method, called *sweating*, brings out their natural sweetness. If they are cooked too quickly and allowed to brown or scorch, they will become bitter. Leeks can be sweated for use in other dishes, or cooked quickly.

Heat 1 tablespoon butter or oil in a saucepan or skillet over medium heat. Add chopped or sliced onions and cook gently, stirring occasionally, or braise slowly over very low heat, covered, for 30 minutes until lightly golden.

To sauté sliced or chopped leeks, heat 1–2 tablespoons butter in a large skillet over medium-high heat. Add the leeks and stir-fry until bright green and just tender, 3–4 minutes. Small whole scallions can be stir-fried the same way.

Stalks and Shoots

Stalks and shoots are vegetable plant stems which contain a high percentage of cellulose fiber. These vegetables – asparagus, celery, cardoon, and artichokes (an edible thistle) – tend to be crisp when raw and highly aromatic when cooked – most have been eaten for hundreds of years.

Asparagus can range from pencil thin to jumbo, extra-thick spears. Fresh-tasting green asparagus is most popular in the United States and Britain. The thick white asparagus preferred by the French and Belgians is milder and slightly softer. Common celery is used as a flavoring in soups, stocks, and stews, but can be eaten raw in salads, used for dipping, or gently braised. Fennel, sometimes called by its Italian name *finocchio*, is a Mediterranean plant with a fresh crunchy texture and anise flavor, ideal for salads and crudités, braising or stir-frying. Cardoon, another Mediterranean vegetable, is more closely related to the artichoke, although its flavor is between artichoke and celery. Tender young artichokes can be cooked and eaten whole, and are very popular in Italian cooking. In large globe artichokes, the choke, or flower, must be discarded.

PREPARING AND COOKING WHOLE ARTICHOKES

Always use a stainless steel knife to prepare artichokes, and rub all cut surfaces with lemon juice to prevent discoloration.

❶ Snap off the stalk close to the base, pulling out any fibers which would extend into the bottom, then trim the base with a knife so it sits flat. Cut off the pointed top and, using kitchen scissors, trim the leaves to remove spines and any brown edges. Separate the leaves and rinse under cold running water. The artichoke is ready to be cooked whole.

❷ Boil a large saucepan of salted water. Add the juice of 1 lemon or 3–4 tablespoons vinegar and the artichoke, upside down, and cover with a heatproof plate or wet cloth to keep it submerged. Simmer until tender, when the stem end can be pierced with a fork or knife tip, 15–25 minutes, depending on size. Drain upside down and cool slightly.

❸ To remove the choke, first grasp the central cone of leaves with your fingers and twist and lift out; reserve the cone of leaves. Using a teaspoon, separate the leaves and scrape out the hairy choke and discard.

❹ Replace the reserved cone of leaves, upside down in the center, and fill it with a favorite dipping

PREPARING AND COOKING ASPARAGUS

Very thin, tender asparagus only needs washing and trimming the stalk ends. Thicker asparagus should be peeled to remove the stringy outer layers and woody stems.

Break each asparagus spear where it snaps easily, then trim all the spears to the same length. Hold a spear just below the tip, flat against the board, and using a vegetable peeler, remove the thick outer layer.

To cook, fill a large skillet with 1 inch water and ½ teaspoon salt. Bring to a boil over medium-high heat. Add the asparagus and simmer 3–4 minutes until tender. Asparagus spears can be also cooked upright in tall asparagus steamers, or stir-fried.

PREPARING AND COOKING CELERY

Celery benefits from lightly peeling to remove the coarsest strings from the outside of the stalks.

Snap the end of a celery stalk, but do not separate it completely; pull off with the strings attached. Alternatively, peel each stalk with a vegetable peeler. For celery hearts, cut lengthwise in half, trimming off any leaves.

To braise slices, simmer with 1 tablespoon butter and 2–3 tablespoons stock or water, 2–3 minutes, until just tender. Cover celery hearts with about 1 cup/ 8 oz water and 1 tablespoon butter, and simmer about 20 minutes.

Grains and Legumes

Grains and legumes should be kept as fresh as possible. Good bright color, plump texture, and a fresh aroma are a good sign. As they age, both grains and legumes require longer cooking. Store them in a cool, dry place in airtight containers.

Rice and Other Grains

The harvesting process dehydrates grains, so they must be cooked in a generous amount of liquid to reabsorb moisture and soften. Water is the most accessible, but stock can be used for savory dishes, while milk is usual for breakfast porridge and rice puddings. Timings vary for different grains, tempered by their age and dryness. Whole grains will need longer cooking than polished or refined varieties. Most grains should be cooked *al dente*, tender but with a slight firmness on the inside; whole grains are a little chewier. Some – such as wild rice – burst when done, but most should hold their shape. Grains can be boiled, steamed, baked, or cooked as pilaff, but whatever method you choose, allow the cooked grain to stand, covered, for about 5 minutes. This allows the individual grains to contract, much like letting meat rest. To separate the grains, toss lightly with a fork. The timings and quantities on page 88 are for long-grain white rice; other grains will have different requirements.

Long grain rice

Basmati

Jasmin

Carolina or American long grain rice

Arborio

Wild rice

A DICTIONARY OF RICE

There are hundreds of kinds of rice, most defined by the size of the grain, some by their origins. Different varieties need different styles of cooking and result in an assortment of flavors and textures. Much long-grain white rice is *converted*: that is, partially steamed to force nutrients from the outer bran into the endosperm so they are maintained when the rice is husked.

Long-grain rice cooks dry and fluffy, providing tender, separate grains. It is 4 to 5 times as long as it is wide. *Carolina*, a long-grain variety grown in the southern states, is also called American long-grain rice. *Basmati*, another long-grain rice is sometimes called "the Champagne of rice." Highly prized for its exotic perfume, it is a staple of Indian cooking, requiring washing before use. *Pecan rice* is a new American long-grain brown rice variety with the flavor of pecans.

Medium-grain rice, such as arborio, is slightly rounder and absorbs a little more liquid than long-grain varieties, producing a slightly more moist, stickier result. But it can be used as long-grain rice. *Valencia*, the Spanish rice traditionally used for *paella*, produces a tender, plump grain, but does not become mushy. It is difficult to find outside Spain. *Sticky rice* or glutinous rice is a medium- to short-grain rice used in Chinese and Japanese cooking, because it is easier to eat with chopsticks.

Thai fragrant rice has a special perfume, and its young, tender grains are much prized by the Thais and Vietnamese.

Wild rice is not a cereal, but an aquatic grass which grows along rivers and lakes on the Canadian-American border. The long, thin black grains have a nutty flavor and chewy texture. It is often mixed with white rice to defray the cost – it is very expensive. It takes 15 to 20 minutes longer than white rice to cook and absorbs about four times its volume in liquid.

Other grains Many other grains can be cooked and eaten like rice; some may absorb more water than white rice. Follow directions on the package.

COOKING RICE AND OTHER GRAINS

TO BOIL
Bring a large pot of water to a boil (about 4 times the amount of water to rice or other grain). Gradually add rice (or other grain) so water continues to boil. Stir once, and continue to boil until it tests tender. Drain in a colander and rinse with hot water.

THE ABSORPTION METHOD
Put water or stock (usually 1½ times the amount of rice) in a medium saucepan and bring to a boil. Add rice and bring back to a boil. Stir, then steam, covered, 18–20 minutes, until water is completely absorbed and rice is tender (about 15 minutes more for brown rice).

TO BAKE
Put the measured rice in an ovenproof baking dish. Pour in 1½ times the amount of boiling water or stock. Stir and cover tightly. Bake in a 350°F oven for about 25 minutes, until the water has been absorbed and rice is tender. (Cook brown rice about 15 minutes longer).

TO STEAM
Line a steamer with dampened cheesecloth. Spread the rice evenly over the surface and place over a pan of simmering water. Cover and steam about 20 minutes, until tender.

THE PILAFF METHOD
Heat a small amount of butter or oil in a saucepan over medium heat. Stir in the rice and cook 2 minutes, until it becomes opaque. Add 1½ times the amount of water or stock to rice. Season with salt and pepper, and stir once. Bring to a boil and cover. Reduce heat and cook 18 to 20 minutes, until tender.

COOKING BULGAR (CRACKED WHEAT): TABBOULEH SALAD

Bulgar is a type of cracked wheat with a nutty flavor, which cooks to a light fluffy texture. Highly nutritious, it is made by steaming wheat berries before drying and cracking them into tiny pieces.

This Middle Eastern favorite can be simmered or cooked by the pilaff method, or steamed like rice. It only needs to be soaked before it is used in tabbouleh, a herb salad of parsley, mint, bulgar, and tomatoes.

INGREDIENTS
½ cup/4 oz bulgar wheat
1 medium red onion, finely chopped
1 cup seeded and chopped tomatoes (peeled if you like)
5 tablespoons chopped Italian flat-leaf parsley (continental)
5 tablespoons chopped fresh mint
½ cup/4 oz virgin olive oil
¼ cup/2 oz freshly squeezed lemon juice

❶ To soak: rinse under cold running water. Turn into a large bowl and cover with twice as much water as bulgar. Allow to stand 1 hour until plump and tender. Add more water if necessary. Drain if too much liquid is added. Fluff with a fork to separate grains.

❷ Stir in the onion, chopped tomatoes, chopped herbs, oil, and lemon juice or vinegar. Season with the salt and black pepper. Garnish with mint leaves and lemon wedges. Serve with black olives. (The salad should look very green, not beige.)

PREPARING AND COOKING COUSCOUS

Couscous is not really a grain, but a tiny pasta. This North African staple is made from semolina (durum wheat), which was traditionally hand-rolled into "grains" that were dampened and coated with flour. This slightly enlarges the grains and helps to keep them separate during cooking. Most of the couscous now available is processed mechanically, replacing the labor-intensive procedure. It simply needs a short soaking, then steaming. This is called *quick-cooking couscous.*

Couscous is the name of a famous North African stew simmered in a special steamer or *couscoussière.*

BUSY COOKS

QUICK-COOKING COUSCOUS
Put 1 tablespoon butter or oil in a saucepan with 1½ cups water or stock. Season with salt, pepper, and any other desired spices or herbs. Bring to a boil and gradually stir in 1 cup couscous. Return to a boil and remove from the heat. Cover and allow to stand about 10 minutes. Fluff with a fork before serving.

Couscous makes a delicious stuffing for poultry and can be soaked and used like bulgar for a tabbouleh-style salad.

1 Put the couscous in a large strainer and rinse under cold running water until the water runs clear. Turn into a bowl and add enough cold water to cover by ½ inch. Allow to stand about 30 minutes. Drain again. (If the couscous is being used for stuffing, proceed as the recipe directs.)

2 To serve the couscous as the main accompaniment, line a colander or flat steamer with dampened cheesecloth and set aside. Rub the drained couscous between your fingers to remove any lumps and put in the colander. Set over a pan of boiling water (or the stew) and steam, uncovered, for about 30 minutes. Serve with the traditional stew or other meats and vegetables.

POLENTA: COOKING POLENTA

Polenta is coarsely ground cornmeal cooked in water or stock to a mushy consistency. Stirred with butter, oil, and/or cheese, and sometimes served with a tomato sauce, it is a popular northern Italian side dish with roast meats, sausages, and stews. it can also be chilled, sliced and fried, or baked.

Polenta must be watched and stirred constantly as it cooks to a thick, creamy mass.

INGREDIENTS
4 cups/2 pints water
1½ teaspoons salt
1 cup polenta
4 tablespoons unsalted butter
3–4 tablespoons freshly grated
    Parmesan cheese

1 Put water and salt in a deep, heavy-based saucepan and bring to a boil. Gradually add polenta in a steady stream, whisking constantly. Stir in half the butter.

2 Reduce heat to low and stir constantly, using a wooden spoon, 15–20 minutes until thickened. The mixture will begin to pull away from the side of the pan. Remove from heat and stir in cheese and remaining butter. Serve immediately as a hot accompaniment.

3 To serve in slices, proceed as above, omitting the butter and cheese, if you like. Then pour the hot polenta into an oiled loaf, cake, or jelly-roll pan, smoothing the top evenly. Cool completely, and chill until firm.

4 Slice or use cutters to make shapes ½ inch thick; broil. If desired, top the broiled polenta slices with crumbled gorgonzola or other strong cheese and continue to broil until the cheese melts. Use broiled polenta slices as a base for tomato or meat sauces or garlicky sautéed mushrooms.

CORN AND CORNMEAL

In many parts of the world, especially in the United States, corn rivals wheat as the most important grain. There are many varieties of corn, including a blue one that originated with Native Americans which has a sweet, earthy taste. It is usually ground like flour and made into tortillas and corn chips.

Cornmeal is finely ground from dried white or yellow corn. Most of it is ground from the kernel after the hull and germ are removed. It is a staple in many parts of the world; it is eaten boiled (4 parts water to 1 part cornmeal) as a breakfast porridge with butter or syrup, or cooled, sliced, and fried as a side dish. It is used in a wide variety of puddings, corn breads, muffins, and tortillas. It also makes a crispy coating for fish. It can be stored for 1 year in a cool, dry place.

Cornstarch is a finely powdered starch ground from corn kernels. It is used as a thickener for sauces, especially in Chinese recipes. It can help "soften" some hard flours; use it to replace 1–2 tablespoons from 1 cup of all-purpose or hard wheat flour to make delicate pastries or shortbread.

Hominy is the dried kernel of hulled corn. It is softened first by soaking, then by long cooking in milk. Thereafter it is treated like cornmeal.

Grits are ground hominy, a fine, white cereal cooked in water to a mushy consistency for breakfast dishes and side dishes. It is very popular in the Southern U.S.

Legumes

Legumes, which include peas, beans, and lentils, are the edible seeds of pod plants. Most commonly sold dried, they are second only to grains as the world's most important foodstuff. High in protein and carbohydrates, they are indispensable in a vegetarian diet. Combined with grains, they form a complete protein. This duo forms the basis of many national dishes, from Mexican beans and rice to Italian pasta and bean soup.

BEAN GLOSSARY

There is a tremendous range of dried beans, peas, and lentils, varying in size, color, and shape. Most need at least 4 hours soaking, but can be left overnight to save time. Soaking is not necessary for lentils or split peas, although it will shorten their cooking time.

Aduki beans A small, sweet, reddish bean used in Asia and called "King of beans" in Japan.
Black beans Also called "turtle beans," these smooth, shiny little black beans, which keep their shape well, are popular for soups and stews.
Black-eyed peas These small, oval, cream-colored beans have a black dot on one side with a small cream dot in the center. They are used in American and African cooking.

Borlotti beans This medium-sized Italian bean is kidney-shaped with a reddish-pink color and tan stripes. It is often used in salads.
Butter beans Also called lima beans, these flat, oval beans are pale green and cook to a soft tender consistency.
Cannellini Also called the *fazolia* bean, this bean is an important ingredient in *minestrone*.

Aduki beans

Black beans

Black-eye beans or peas

Borlotti beans

Butter beans

Cannellini

BEAN GLOSSARY CONTINUED

Garbanzo beans Also called chickpeas or *ceci* in Italian. Roundish, wrinkled, pea-shaped beans, they need long soaking and cooking. They are popular in Middle Eastern dishes.

Dried peas These round field peas are a staple in the Mediterranean. They vary in color from blue-gray to brown-black.

Split peas are dried peas, split in half when their seed coat peels away. Yellow split peas are milder than green ones; they are also sweeter and less starchy than whole peas, and are the main ingredient in Ham and Pea Soup.

Flageolet beans These mild, pale green beans often complement roast lamb in France.

Haricot beans Also known as the great northern bean, this is a white bean with a mild flavor and mealy texture, which holds its shape well. Widely used, it is slightly larger than the Boston or navy bean, or the pearl haricot. All can be used interchangeably in Boston Baked Beans.

Kidney beans Smooth, shiny, kidney-shaped beans can be red, white, or black. Most common is the hearty red kidney bean or red bean used in Chili-con-carne.

Lentils The smaller the better, these green, red, or brown flat, dried seeds, need little or no soaking. The deep, greenish gray-blue Puy lentil keeps its shape as a hot accompaniment or in salads. The red or yellow lentil is used in Indian *dal*.

Pinto beans Pretty beige, oval beans speckled with pink, these small beans can be substituted for red kidney beans.

Soya beans These small, round Asian beans can be black or beige. Rich in carbohydrates, they form the base of many other products, from flours to milk to soy sauce.

Garbanzo beans

Dried peas

Flageolot beans

Haricot beans

Lentils

Pinto beans

Split peas

Kidney beans

Soya beans

SOAKING AND COOKING LEGUMES

With the exception of lentils and split peas, dried legumes need soaking to shorten the cooking time, make them more digestible, and prevent splitting. Garbanzo and soy beans are especially dense and need slightly longer soaking.

❶ Pick over the beans or peas and rinse under cold running water. Put them in a large bowl, cover by at least 1 inch cold water, and soak for 6 to 8 hours or overnight. Drain and rinse well.

❷ Alternatively, put legumes in a large pot, cover with cold water, and bring to a boil. Boil for 2 minutes, remove from heat, cover, and stand for 1 hour. Drain and rinse.

❸ Put beans in a large saucepan or Dutch oven and cover with cold water (3 parts water to 1 part legumes). Bring to a boil over medium-high heat. Boil rapidly for 10 minutes. Simmer 45 minutes to 1 hour, depending on the type and age of the legume.

❹ Test the beans for doneness; the interior should be soft but the skin firm.

BEAN KNOW-HOW

Most legumes need to be *boiled rapidly for the first ten minutes* to remove toxins on the skin. Reduce the heat and simmer gently for the remainder of the cooking time. Lentils and split peas do not need this treatment. Simply bring to a boil, reduce the heat, and simmer.

Salt or other seasonings should not be added to legumes until they are cooked, as they toughen the skin. Add about 10 minutes before the end of cooking time to improve flavor.

Pasta, Noodles, and Dumplings

Although pasta has been a household ingredient for years, it became seriously trendy in the early 1980s. Served in every restaurant and widely available in supermarkets, Italian delicatessens, and specialty stores, pasta is probably one of the world's most popular foods. Noodles are increasingly popular, especially with the explosion of interest in foods from the Far East. Dumplings are a traditional, warming and filling accompaniment to stews and desserts.

Pasta

Made from an unleavened combination of flour and liquid (either water or eggs) pasta is a versatile, inexpensive, nutritious food, a well-known staple since ancient times throughout Italy, the Middle East, and Asia. After industrial production of pasta began in Naples, Italy, during the 18th century, the popularity of pasta began to spread worldwide.

There are two basic types of pasta; *dried* and *fresh*. When buying dried pasta, look for the worlds "durum wheat," "pure semolina," or "pasta di semola di grano duro" on the package. Dried pasta is available in countless shapes and sizes, as well as in many flavors, such as spinach, beet, herb, and garlic; they are almost always known by their Italian names. Dried packaged "egg noodles" or Pennsylvania Dutch noodles are one of the few widely available dried egg noodles. Dried pasta keeps indefinitely if stored in a cool, dry place.

Fresh pasta has become popular and very chic in the last few years. Made from flour, eggs, and sometimes a little oil and salt for flavor, it is rolled out by hand or machine, then cut into noodles, shaped into bows, spirals, or other "fancies," or filled with a stuffing. Fresh pasta is usually made with a strong flour or a special pasta flour, as homemade pasta made with semolina is almost impossible to roll out thinly and is difficult to handle. It can be made by hand or in a food processor. A pasta machine is invaluable for kneading, rolling, and cutting homemade pasta.

PASTA GLOSSARY

There are hundreds of pasta shapes, both dried and fresh.

Lasagne Broad noodles at least 2 inches wide, available dried or fresh. The cooked noodle is layered with meat or tomato sauce, cheese and vegetables, or seafood, and baked in a casserole.

Fusilli tricolori Corkscrew-shaped noodles about 2 inches long (they can be spaghetti-length).

Farfalle Butterfly-shaped noodles about 2 inches long and ³/₄ inch wide. Pinched in at the middle.

Pipe rigate Small, short, ridged pasta shapes.

Conchiglie Small, shell shaped.

Penne rigate Sometimes called quills, 2 inch long ridged tubes cut on the diagonal.

Egg campanelle Use with a chunky sauce.

Tagliatelle (paglia e fieno). A ribbon-like flat noodle about ¹/₄ inch wide.

Cannelloni Pasta tubes 3–4 inches long, generally filled, covered with sauce, and baked.

Spirali Also called rotelle, these are short, 2 inch long, corkscrew-shaped pasta.

Macaroni Sometimes elbow-shaped, these are short, hollow tubes, baked with a cheese sauce.

Spaghetti Long, thin rod-like pasta made from white or wholewheat flour. Thin spaghetti is called spaghettini.

Ravioli Usually fresh, square-shaped pasta stuffed with a meat, cheese, or vegetable filling.

Tortelloni Fresh white or spinach pasta filled with cheese, meat, or other fillings, and formed into a ring-shaped dumpling.

Capelli d'Angelo Very fine, long strands of pasta, sometimes called "angel-hair" pasta.

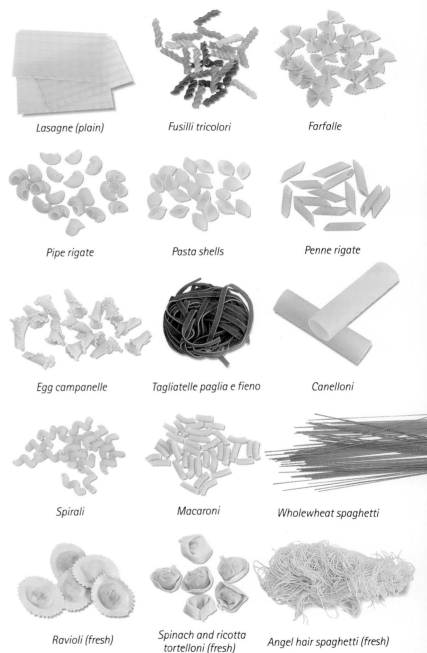

Lasagne (plain) Fusilli tricolori Farfalle

Pipe rigate Pasta shells Penne rigate

Egg campanelle Tagliatelle paglia e fieno Canelloni

Spirali Macaroni Wholewheat spaghetti

Ravioli (fresh) Spinach and ricotta tortelloni (fresh) Angel hair spaghetti (fresh)

MAKING PASTA DOUGH: BASIC EGG PASTA

As with bread and pastry doughs, the amount of liquid the flour will hold depends on the type of flour.

INGREDIENTS
2 cups/10 oz all-purpose flour or pasta flour ("type 00")
1 teaspoon salt
1 tablespoon oil (optional)
3 medium eggs, lightly beaten

1 Put flour and salt in a bowl or on a work surface. Stir to blend. Make a well in the center, into which add the eggs, and, if using, oil.

2 With a fork or your fingertips, gradually incorporate the flour into the eggs until a soft dough forms. If dough is very sticky, work in a little more flour.

3 Knead the dough on the work surface for about 8–10 minutes, until it is smooth and elastic. Add a little flour, if necessary.

4 Cover the dough with an upturned bowl. Allow to rest about 20 minutes. Alternatively, put the dough into a bowl, cover with plastic wrap, and refrigerate overnight or until ready to roll and shape.

COLORED PASTA

Dried pastas are available in a variety of colors, but remember if coloring pasta at home, you may need to add a little more flour to the basic dough to compensate for the extra moisture.

Green pasta Add *12 oz cooked fresh spinach* or *swiss chard*, squeezed dry, and finely chopped with the *eggs*.

Red pasta Add *1–2 tablespoons tomato paste* or *finely chopped sun-dried tomatoes* with the *eggs*; add *4 tablespoons carrot* or *red bell pepper purée* with the *eggs*.

Beet pasta Add *1½ tablespoons beet purée* to the *eggs*.

Fresh herb pasta Add *2 tablespoons finely chopped parsley, basil, tarragon,* or *cilantro* with the *eggs*; if you like, add *1–2 cloves of finely chopped garlic* with the *eggs*.

Lemon pasta Add *1½ tablespoons grated zest* and *½ teaspoon lemon juice* with the *eggs*.

Saffron or yellow pasta Add *½ teaspoon ground saffron* to the *flour* or steep a few *saffron threads* in *1 tablespoon hot water*; add with the *eggs*.

Wholewheat pasta Replace *2–3 oz white flour* with the same quantity *wholewheat flour*.

ROLLING AND CUTTING PASTA DOUGH BY HAND

Cut the dough into thirds or quarters. Work with one piece at a time, keeping the remaining pieces covered to prevent drying out.

1 Using a long pasta rolling pin or extra-long rolling pin, begin from the center, rolling out the dough on a lightly floured surface to a thickness of ⅛ inch – or thinner, if possible. If the dough becomes too elastic to handle, cover for a few minutes with a damp dishtowel and let it rest.

2 If making filled pasta shapes, cut the shapes immediately while the dough is still soft and pliable. If hand-cutting noodles, dust lightly with flour and allow to dry slightly for about 10–20 minutes. (If machine cutting, allow to dry only about 5–10 minutes.)

TO CUT NOODLES BY HAND
1 Loosely roll up dough and cut crosswise: ⅛ inch for fettuccine, ¼ inch for tagliatelle, ½ inch for pappardelle or wide egg noodles.

2 Unroll the noodles and spread on a clean dishtowel; sprinkle with a little flour or semolina and toss to prevent sticking. Alternatively, hang noodles on a special pasta drying rack, towel rack, or broom handle propped on two chair backs. Dry up to 2–3 hours before cooking. If not cooking immediately, refrigerate in layers, dusted with flour or semolina, in an airtight container.

ROLLING AND CUTTING PASTA BY MACHINE

If you intend to make pasta regularly, it is worth investing in a pasta machine. In addition to rolling and cutting, it can knead the dough evenly beforehand.

1 To knead dough, set the machine rollers to the widest setting. Flour both rollers and the dough. Flatten the dough slightly before feeding it through the rollers, while turning the handle.

2 Fold the dough in thirds, folding the top third over, then the bottom third up over the top.

3 Feed it through again, open-side first through the rollers. Continue rolling and folding 6–8 times, flouring dough and rollers as necessary. This completes the kneading process.

4 To roll and flatten the dough, narrow the rollers by one notch. Feed the dough strip through. Now do not fold the dough; narrow the rollers by one notch and feed the dough strip through again. Continue rolling and narrowing the gap between rollers until the dough is thin enough to be cut, about 1/8 inch or thinner. (The dough will be about a yard long.) Spread the dough on a surface, dust with flour, and allow to dry slightly, about 10–15 minutes. This will help prevent the dough from sticking to the rollers when cutting.

5 To cut the dough, lightly flour a baking sheet or dishcloth and set under the machine. Move the setting to the cutting roller or fit the cutting roller as directed. Feed the dough strip through, letting the cut noodles fall loosely onto the baking sheet or towel. Dust the noodles with a little more flour or semolina and store as for hand-cut noodles.

TO CUT LASAGNE STRIPS

Using a chef's knife or pasta wheel, cut the long dough strip into 10 x 12-inch rectangles, or cut to fit a specific baking dish as recipe directs. To cut for cannelloni, cut into 3 x 5-inch rectangles. Dry slightly, as for noodles.

TO MAKE FILLED PASTA

Prepare the filling and roll the pasta extra thin, at least 1/6 inch. Filled shapes will have a double thickness of pasta, so it must be rolled thin. About 1 pound stuffing will fill about 25–30 shapes.

2 Dip a pastry brush or your fingers sparingly in water and moisten the pasta dough around the filling.

4 Using a chef's knife or pasta or pizza wheel, first cut vertical, then horizontal lines between the filled squares. Using a fork, press to seal the edges of the filled pasta squares. Sprinkle with a little semolina to prevent sticking.

RAVIOLI

1 Lay a dough strip on a lightly floured surface and cut crosswise in half. Onto one half, drop 1/2 teaspoon of the filling in vertical rows about 1 1/2 inch apart.

3 Lay the other half of the dough strip on top. Press the dough sheets together between the mounds of filling.

5 Alternatively, cut the ravioli with a round cutter or other shape and sprinkle as in step 4. Allow to dry slightly before cooking, or store up to 1 day as for fresh-cut noodles.

TO MAKE FILLED PASTA CONTINUED

TORTELLONI

1 Use a 3-inch round cutter to make as many circles from the rolled-out pasta dough as possible. Put a teaspoon of filling in the center of each and brush the dough edge with water.

2 Fold one side of the dough over to enclose the filling, making a half-moon shape. Press the edges together to seal well.

3 Moisten the ends on one side of the half moon. Curve the dough around your index finger, allowing the top curved edge to bend over the filled center forming a pleat. Pinch the moistened pointed ends together to seal them.

STORING PASTA

DRYING PASTA If fresh pasta is not used within an hour or two of making, it should be dried completely or it will become moldy. Hang pasta for several hours on a special drying rack, towel rack, or a broom handle propped between 2 chairs.

NOODLES Curl cut noodles into nests while still soft. Lay on a floured baking sheet or dishtowel to dry thoroughly. Arrange noodles in layers in a plastic box or container, sprinkled with semolina or cornmeal. Use wax paper or baking parchment to separate layers and prevent sticking. Refrigerate up to 3 days.

FILLED PASTA Store filled pasta shapes on a baking sheet or in layers, sprinkled with semolina or cornmeal, for up to 1 day.

COOKING PASTA

Fresh pasta and dried pasta are cooked the same way, in plenty of boiling salted water. Allow about 7 pints of water for each pound of pasta. Use about 1 tablespoon salt for each pound of pasta. If you like, add a tablespoon of oil to the water when it comes to a boil; some cooks say it helps to prevent the pasta from sticking to itself.

1 Bring a large pot of salted water to a rapid boil over high heat. Add the pasta and bring the water back to a boil as quickly as possible, stirring occasionally.

2 If cooking spaghetti, hold the spaghetti in one hand and push one end into the water slowly; it will begin to bend as it softens. Gradually push it completely into the water, stirring with a long-handled fork to separate.

3 When the water comes back to a boil, reduce the heat slightly and cook at a gentle boil. Follow the recommended cooking times on the package for dried pasta, but begin testing at the minimum end of the cooking time range. Thin pastas, like angel-hair, can be cooked in 3 minutes, while rigatoni could take as long as 12 minutes. To test, use a slotted spoon to lift a piece of pasta out of the water. Run it under cold water and bite into it; it should be *al dente* or "firm to the tooth." Or, cut in half with a small sharp knife. It should look completely cooked with no opaque or uncooked dough in the center.

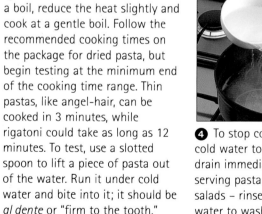

4 To stop cooking, add a cup of cold water to the pasta pot. Then drain immediately in a colander. If serving pasta cold – as for pasta salads – rinse under cold running water to wash away the starch and prevent further cooking. Toss in a little oil to prevent sticking. If using in a baked casserole, like lasagne, undercook slightly.

5 Fresh pasta noodles cook in under a minute. Drop into the boiling water; they are cooked as soon as they float to the surface. Stuffed shapes take between 7–9 minutes, as there are two layers of pasta.

Noodles and Dumplings

Asian and some other cultures use their pasta in the form of noodles. Noodles can be fresh or dried, with or without egg, made from wheat flour, soybean flour, or rice flour. Most are boiled like Mediterranean pasta, but some require soaking to soften for eating or frying.

Dumplings are small rounds of dough, sometimes leavened, poached in a simmering liquid such as water, stock, or milk. Although generally easy to make, dumplings can be tricky to cook. If the recipe directs cooking covered, do not be tempted to uncover – when re-covering causes the temperature to rise again, there is a risk they will overcook. Allow room for dumplings to expand and keep them at a simmer; boiling hard could cause them to break up.

NOODLE GLOSSARY

Cellophane noodles Made from mung-bean flour. Used in most oriental cuisines. *Harusame*, Japanese cellophane noodles, are made from rice flour. They need to be soaked before cooking.

Egg noodles Fresh egg noodles made from wheatflour and egg. They are the most commonly used noodles, from soups to stir-fries.

Rice noodles Thin white noodles, mostly sold dried in bundles. They need to be soaked for about 2 hours before boiling.

Rice papers Thin, dry, translucent circles used to make Thai- and Vietnamese-style spring rolls.

Rice sticks Ribbon-like rice noodles. Use in fried dishes.

Soba noodles Thin, flat, usually buckwheat noodles popular in Japanese "fast foods," like noodle soups. Can also be served cold with a dipping sauce.

Somen Fine, shiny, white Japanese wheatflour noodles which cook in 2–3 minutes. Served cold with a dipping sauce.

Udon Long, thin, ribbon-like Japanese wheatflour noodles.

Wheat noodles Chinese wheatflour noodles, made without eggs.

Wonton wrappers Wafer-thin wheatflour squares, about 3 inches square, sold fresh or frozen.

Yifu noodles Round yellow egg noodles, woven into a round cake. For use in soups and stir-fries.

Egg noodles

Rice noodles

Rice paper

Somen

Yifu noodles

MATZO BALLS (KNEIDLACH)

INGREDIENTS
4 eggs, lightly beaten
5 tablespoons margarine or vegetable fat, softened almost to melting
¼ cup/2 oz chicken stock or water
1 teaspoon salt
¼ teaspoon pepper
Pinch of cinnamon or nutmeg
1 cup/4 oz matzo meal

❶ Beat eggs with the almost melted margarine or vegetable fat, the chicken stock or water, and the salt, pepper, and cinnamon.

❷ Stir in matzo meal until well blended. Cover and refrigerate about 1 hour (this allows the matzo meal to absorb the liquid and swell.)

❸ Using wet hands, shape the dough into ¾ inch balls and drop into simmering soup or water. Cover and simmer about 20 minutes. Serve in the soup or add to other soups.

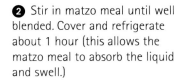

Soba noodles

Wonton wrappers

Pastry

Pastry is rich, unleavened dough made with flour, some kind of fat, and usually a liquid to bind the two together. All cooks aspire to making light, tender, flaky pastry. To achieve this goal, it is important to understand what each ingredient does and how it reacts, then to follow some basic rules in making and handling the dough.

Making Pastry

There are three basic kinds of pastry – plain pastry, of which shortcrust or pie crust is the best known; puff pastry, the famous *pâte feuilletée* of *mille-feuille* (napoleons); and choux pastry, the basis for cream puffs and profiteroles.

Be careful not to overwork the dough or the pastry will be too tough. "Relaxing" the dough is essential for all pastries. Chilling the dough makes it easier to manage. Keep the ingredients and pastry chilled between each step of preparation for light, crispy pastry. With rich pastry, soften the dough at room temperature for 10–15 minutes, and lightly flour the rolling pin and work surface, for easier rolling.

PASTRY INGREDIENTS

Although there are limited ingredients in pastry, they can vary greatly, giving a variety of results. In pastry making, *measuring accurately is paramount*, and ingredients should be weighed rather than measured by volume, if possible.

Flour Flour is the most important ingredient. A soft wheat flour is best for pastry. Hard flours produce a firm, harder dough. All-purpose flour is used throughout the U.S. Pastry flour (not to be confused with cake flour) is ideal, but difficult to find. European and British flours tend to be milled from softer wheats, ideal for pastry. Wholewheat or rye flours produce a slightly heavier result. Use more white flour to wholewheat or other flours for easier handling.

Fat Fat provides the shortness in pastry, as well as its richness and flavor. The normal proportion is usually half fat to flour. The more fat the dough contains, the more difficult it will be to handle, so be sure to chill it after every stage.

Liquids Most pastry is bound with water, although milk or other liquids can be used. Use the minimum amount of liquid, as too much can make a sticky, hard-to-handle dough and a tough pastry. The water should be iced or very cold. The normal proportion is about 1 teaspoon water per ounce of flour, but this will vary if whole eggs, yolks, or other liquids are used.

Eggs Eggs or egg yolks are added to pastry for richness and flavor, and because they help bind the ingredients. Some rich European-style doughs use only yolks with the fat and flour.

Salt and sugar Salt, as in many other preparations, helps to bring out the flavor of the other ingredients. Sugar sweetens pastry and gives it a crisper texture.

SHORTCRUST PASTRY (PATE BRISEE)

Pâte Brisée, a basic pie crust, produces a firm, flaky crust which is supportive, yet tender. *Brisée* in French means broken; in this dough the flour and fats are "broken together" or rubbed in, as we say. Use half fat and half butter if you prefer, but remember the white fat will make the pastry shorter and more difficult to handle. If, after adding the liquid, the dough becomes sticky, refrigerate it. Sifting the flour is not necessary but can help lighten the pastry. The amount of pastry below is for a 9–10-inch pie or tart pan.

INGREDIENTS
1¼ cups/6 oz all-purpose flour
½ teaspoon salt
1 teaspoon sugar, optional
6 tablespoons cold unsalted butter or margarine, cut into small pieces
2 tablespoons cold margarine or white vegetable fat, cut into small pieces
2–4 tablespoons ice water

❶ Sift the flour, salt, and sugar, if using, into a large bowl. Sprinkle the pieces of fat over the flour mixture. Cut in the fat until the mixture forms coarse crumbs. Do not overwork or allow to become warm.

❷ Sprinkle about 2 tablespoons water over the flour-crumb mixture and toss lightly with a fork. Gather together any pieces of dough which have "clumped" together. Add a little more water to the dry crumbs and toss again, continuing until the mixture is moist enough to stick together when pinched between your thumb and index finger.

❸ Gather the dough into a rough ball and put onto a sheet of plastic wrap. Press the dough into a flat disk shape about 1 inch thick. Wrap tightly and refrigerate at least 1 hour or overnight.

RICH SHORTCRUST PASTRY (PATE BRISEE RICHE)

INGREDIENTS
1¼ cups/6 oz all-purpose flour
½ teaspoon salt
1–2 teaspoons superfine sugar (optional)
1 stick/4 oz cold unsalted butter, cut into small pieces
1 egg yolk, beaten with 2 tablespoons water

VARIATIONS
Light wholewheat crust Use ¾ cup/4 oz all-purpose flour, ½ cup/3 oz wholewheat flour, ½ teaspoon salt, 3 tablespoons cold unsalted butter, cut up, 1 tablespoon white vegetable fat or margarine, and egg yolk beaten with 2 tablespoons ice water.

Light nut crust Add 2–3 tablespoons finely chopped nuts to the flour.

Extra-sweet tart crust This rich, melting pastry can be tricky to handle; chill if it becomes too sticky. If it is too difficult to roll out, pat it into a pie plate or tart pan using flour-dipped fingers.

Use 1 cup/5 oz all-purpose flour, ½ teaspoon salt, 4–5 tablespoons confectioner's sugar, 1 stick/4 oz cold unsalted butter, cut into small pieces, 3 egg yolks beaten with 1 tablespoon ice water and ½ teaspoon vanilla extract.

Rich nut crust Ideal for custards and cooked fillings, this dough can be pressed straight into the pan without rolling. Put 2 sticks/ 8 oz room-temperature unsalted butter, 1 lightly beaten egg, 1 teaspoon vanilla or almond extract (optional), 1 cup/5 oz all-purpose flour, ½ teaspoon salt, 1–2 tablespoons sugar, and 1 cup/4 oz finely chopped walnuts, pecans, almonds, hazelnuts or macadamias into the bowl of a

food processor fitted with the metal blade. Using the pulse button, process until well-blended and smooth. Alternatively beat in a large bowl with an electric mixer until well-blended.

Crumb crust Popular for cheesecakes and icecream pies, this is easy to make. Put 1½ cups/4 oz crumbled graham

crackers or other cookies in the bowl of a food processor and process until fine crumbs form. Add 6 tablespoons melted butter and 1–2 tablespoons sugar (optional) and process to blend. Press onto a springform pan or pie plate and chill.

BUSY COOKS

The food processor is the answer to your prayers if you have warm hands, a heavy touch, or just don't have the knack – just be careful not to overprocess. Sweeter doughs, especially, benefit from the food processor.

❶ Put the flour, salt, and sugar into the bowl of a food processor fitted with the metal blade. Process 5 seconds to blend. Sprinkle the fat over the flour mixture and, using the pulse button, process until the mixture resembles coarse crumbs.

❷ Remove the cover and sprinkle 2 tablespoons of the water over the flour mixture. Using the pulse button, process 10–15 seconds until the mixture just begins to hold together – do not overprocess. Test the dough by pinching between your fingers. If the dough is too crumbly, add a little more water, little by little, and pulse again. Do not allow dough to form into a ball or add too much water, or the pastry will be tough. Turn dough onto a sheet of plastic wrap and continue with step 3 as above.

ROLLING PIECRUST PASTRY: TO FORM A DOUGH CIRCLE

For rich pastry soften the dough at room temperature for 10–15 minutes. Lightly flour the work surface and the rolling pin.

❶ Use a lightly floured rolling pin to press a row of parallel grooves into the dough circle. Turn the dough 45°, lightly flouring the surface underneath. Press another row of parallel grooves. Continue rotating and pressing the dough until it is about ½ inch thick.

❷ Beginning from the center, lightly roll out the dough to the far edge, but do not actually roll over the edge. Return to the center and roll to the nearest edge, but do not roll over the edge. Rotate the dough 45° and continue rolling until the dough is about ⅛-inch thick and forms a circle about 12 inches. Lightly flour the surface and the rolling pin as needed.

❸ Use a small pastry brush to remove excess flour from the dough. Patch any tears with a small piece of moistened dough.

❹ As the dough gets bigger, fold it in half or quarters to rotate, or roll it over the rolling pin to dust the surface with flour; this avoids stretching or tearing very fragile doughs.

TO FORM A DOUGH CIRCLE CONTINUED

5 Use a tart pan or overturned pie plate as a guide to trim the dough 2 inches larger all around than the pan or plate.

TO FORM A SQUARE
Proceed as for a dough circle, but rotate the dough 90° instead of 45° when pressing in the grooves. This will cause the dough to elongate to fill a square pan.

TO FREEZE ROLLED-OUT PASTRY

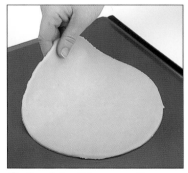

1 Carefully slide onto a flat baking sheet and open-freeze until very firm. Slide the frozen dough shape onto freezer paper, wrap tightly, and freeze.

2 Or, freeze several with layers of freezer paper between each. Defrost in the refrigerator overnight or for several hours at room temperature before using.

LINING A TART PAN OR PIE PLATE

Pie plates have sloped sides and a flattened lip or rim at the edge, making them more suitable for decorative edges. Traditional tart or quiche pans are shallow, straight-sided pans with no lip or rim. They usually have a removable bottom and fluted sides which give the characteristic scalloped edge and allow the tart to be removed for presentation with minimum disruption. Flan rings, generally used by professionals, are usually smooth-sided rings set onto a heavy baking sheet which forms its base.

Use dull-metal, non-stick glass pans; shiny metal reflects the heat and inhibits proper browning. Butter-rich doughs do not usually stick, but spray the pan with a vegetable cooking spray or brush with a little oil as a precaution.

1 To transfer rolled-out dough to a pan, set the rolling pin on the near edge of the pastry circle, square, or rectangle. Fold the edge of the pastry over the rolling pin, then continue rolling the dough loosely around the pin.

2 Hold the far edge of the dough and rolling pin over the far edge of the pan and gently unroll the dough, centering it as much as possible and allowing it to settle into the pan without stretching or pulling.

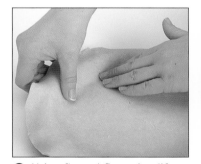

3 Alternatively, lightly fold the dough into quarters. Center the point of the folded dough in the pan and lower it in. Unfold the dough without stretching or pulling.

4 Using floured fingertips, lift the outside edge of the dough and ease into the bottom and side of the pan, allowing any excess to overhang the edge. Press onto the bottom and into side and corners of the pan or plate.

5 To finish lining a tart pan, press the overhang slightly toward the center and roll the rolling pin over the edge. Press the dough against the side. Prick over the bottom with a fork and refrigerate for 1 hour, or freeze 20 minutes, before using.

LINING A TART PAN OR PIE PLATE CONTINUED

6 To finish lining a pie plate, use kitchen scissors to trim the overhang ½–1 inch beyond the edge of the rim, depending on the decorative edge to be used. Make a decorative edge (page 103) and prick the bottom, unless baking with a liquid filling. Refrigerate for 1 hour, or freeze 20 minutes, before using.

TARTLET PANS
To line tartlet pans larger than 2 inches, follow the instructions for lining a tart pan. This should ensure enough pastry and high enough edge to support any fillings.

FOR A TWO-CRUST PIE
1 Line the pie plate as on page 101, using half the dough. Trim the dough even with the rim. Spoon in the filling as directed and brush the rim of the pastry with a little water. Roll out the remaining pastry to a circle at least 1 inch larger than the pie plate. Roll around the rolling pin and,

PETIT-FOUR CASES
1 For *petit-four* cases or very small tartlet pans less than 2 inches, arrange the pans very close together on a work surface. Roll the pastry over a rolling pin and unroll over the pans, allowing

centering it over the pie, unroll the dough over it. Press the edges to seal, then trim the upper edge to within ½ inch of the rim. Fold the overhang under the lower dough edge and press together to seal.

2 Press the edge against the rim of the dish for a flat edge, or pinch up to form a stand-up edge, which can be crimped. Make a decorative edge and slash the top with a sharp knife to allow steam to escape. Decorate if you like. Brush the top with an egg wash and bake as directed.

the pastry to drape into them. Roll the rolling pin over them to cut off excess pastry

2 Using a floured thumb or ball of excess pastry, press the pastry into the bottom and up the side of the pans. Prick the bottoms with a fork and refrigerate for 1 hour, or freeze 20 minutes.

FINISHING THE EDGE

A traditional tart or quiche edge is left plain or finished with simple crimping. An open-faced, two-crust, or covered pie allows for a variety of decorative finishes. To make a decorative-edge, press the rim up to form a stand-up edge.

SIMPLE CRIMPED OR FLUTED EDGE
Pinch the stand-up pastry edge between the thumb and side of the knuckle of the index finger. Place the thumb in the groove left by the index finger and repeat all around the edge.

ROPE EDGE
Pinch pastry as above, but position fingers at a sharper angle to the edge and twist toward the center of the pan.

SHARP FLUTE
Place the left index finger against the inside of the stand-up edge; with the right thumb and index finger, pinch pastry against that point. Repeat every ½ inch around the edge. For a sharper flute, use a star-shaped or other sharp-edged cutter against the inside edge; this gives a more defined look.

SIMPLE FORK EDGE
Flatten the stand-up edge against the rim of the pan and press firmly and evenly with the prongs of a flour-dipped fork around the edge.

CUT-OUT EDGES
Flatten the stand-up edge evenly against the rim of the pan. Using a small pastry cutter, cut out decorative shapes such as hearts, squares, triangles, or leaves from rolled-out pastry trimmings.

DECORATIVE LEAVES
Leaves can be cut from the trimmings by hand. Using a paring knife, cut out a free-form leaf shape and lightly score lines on the surface to effect the leaf veins. Moisten the edge of the pastry and press the cutout shapes against the edge, over-lapping them slightly to cover rim completely. Press gently to secure.

RIBBON EDGE
Flatten the stand-up edge evenly against the rim of the pan. Roll out the pastry trimmings into a rectangular shape and cut out long, ¾-inch strips. Moisten the edge and press the end of one strip to the edge to secure, twist the strip around itself to form a curl, and press to the edge. Continue around the edge, twisting and pressing until edge is covered. Join strips by overlapping.

BRAIDED EDGE
Flatten the stand-up edge evenly against the rim of the pan. Roll out the pastry trimmings into a rectangular shape. Using a straight edge and sharp knife, cut out long, ¼-inch strips and carefully braid groups of 3 strips together. Moisten the edge of the pastry and place a braided strip on the edge, guiding it around the rim of the pan. Two or three braided strips may be necessary. Join them by slightly overlapping to cover the rim completely. Press gently to secure.

MAKING A LATTICE TOP

A woven-lattice top makes an interesting and stylish top for a 2-crust pie. Make enough pastry for a 2-crust pie for a close-woven top. For the lattice-style decoration, the re-rolled trimmings will probably be enough.

❶ Fill the bottom of the lined pie plate as directed. Roll out the second half of the pastry to a round at least 1 inch larger than the pie plate. Using a straight edge and a sharp knife or pastry wheel, cut as many ½-inch strips as possible.

❷ Lay about half the strips in parallel rows across the filled pie, using the longer strips for the center section. Keep them as straight and even as possible.

❸ Fold back every other strip to the center of the pie. Lay one long strip across the center of the pie at right angles over the unfolded strips, or if you prefer, at 45° angles to them (this will create a diamond-shaped lattice). Unfold the folded-back strips.

❹ Fold back the alternate strips which were not folded the first time. Lay another long strip across the flat strips parallel to the first, about ½ inch away.

MAKING A LATTICE TOP CONTINUED

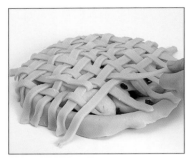

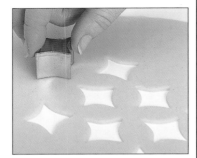

5 Continue folding the alternate original strips and laying on the new ones, until half the pie is covered with a woven lattice. Turn the pie and continue in the same way, weaving the second half.

6 Brush the edge of the bottom pastry and press the pastry strips against the edge to attach them firmly. Trim the strips even with the rim and finish the edge as directed.

MOCK-LATTICE OR CUTOUT TOP
A mock-lattice is easier to make. Roll out the dough for the pie top as directed. Using a small pastry cutter (heart or diamonds are pretty) begin by cutting the shape at the center, then continue outward toward the edge, until an all-over pattern is created. Carefully transfer the top onto pie and continue as before.

MAKING EGG WASH OR GLAZE

All pastries look more attractive if glazed. The glaze adds color and a glossy shine to the surface. A wash or glaze can also be brushed onto a hot, blind-baked tart shell to act as a protective layer before adding a moist filling.

Beat a *whole egg* or *1 egg yolk* with a *tablespoon of water* and a *pinch of salt*. Strain into a small bowl and use to glaze all pastries.

Egg glaze can be used to seal the tops of pie crusts or to help decorations stick to the surface. Do not allow glaze to drip down the sides onto a dish or baking sheet, as it could prevent pastry from rising and make it stick to the baking sheet. When scoring pastry tops, glaze first so the glaze doesn't fill in the slashes and stick them together.

BAKING BLIND

Blind baking, or prebaking prevents the piecrust pastry from becoming soggy and allows the base to cook evenly and completely. Complete baking is necessary for an uncooked filling and partially blind-baking is recommended when a liquid, creamy, or custard-based filling is cooked in the pastry shell. Use dried beans, rice, or ceramic pastry weights to prevent the pastry from puffing and shrinking.

1 Set the tart pan or pie plate on a piece of baking parchment or foil and draw a circle 3 inches larger than the pan or plate. Be sure to prick the bottom of the dough.

2 Fold the paper or foil in half and lay it across the center of the lined pan or plate. Unfold it and press onto the bottom and into the edge of the dough.

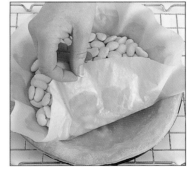

3 Fill with dried beans, rice, or pastry weights, spreading them evenly over the bottom and against the side of the dough. This blind filling can be cooled and used again and again.

4 To partially blind-bake pastry, bake in a 400°F oven for 15–20 minutes, until the pastry is set and rim looks dry and just golden. Remove to a wire rack to cool and remove the paper and weights. The pastry case is then ready for filling and baking.

5 To completely bake, bake in a 400°F oven for 10–12 minutes. Remove to a heatproof surface or rack and carefully remove the paper and weights. Gently prick the bottom again and return to the oven for 5–10 minutes longer, until the bottom looks set and dry and is lightly colored. Remove to a wire rack to cool completely before filling as recipe directs.

PUFF PASTRY

Puff pastry, French *pâte feuilletée*, is probably the most stylish and elegant pastry. Made from the same basic ingredients as other pastries, puff pastry is much richer in butter. The butter is incorporated, not by rubbing in, but by layering it through a series of turns and rollings. When baked, the melting butter and steam which is released causes the dough to rise and separate into hundreds of airy layers.

Classic puff pastry is not actually difficult to handle once the principles are understood; however, it is time-consuming. First a basic dough, called the *détrempe* (dampened-base dough)

is made, then rested to relax any gluten which develops. The butter is then beaten and worked until pliable, and, when it is the same temperature as the *détrempe*, the butter is wrapped in the dough and rolled to a long rectangle. It is folded and rolled six times to incorporate the butter and distribute it evenly within the dough. Puff pastry is used for tarts, *mille-feuilles* (napoleons), *vol-au-vents*, *bouchées* ("little mouthfuls"), *feuilletées* (pastry cases), and many savory cookies.

There are several ways of making mock puff pastry, which achieve similar effects with much less effort.

MOCK PUFF PASTRY

INGREDIENTS
14 tablespoons unsalted butter
2 cups less 1 tablespoon/10 oz all-purpose flour
1 tablespoon cornstarch
1 teaspoon salt
½–¾ cup/4–6 fl oz very cold whipping cream or half cream and half ice water

❶ Cut the butter into tiny (about ¼-inch) squares. Set on a plate, spread evenly, and freeze for 30 minutes. While the butter freezes, chill your work surface with a roasting pan or baking tray filled with ice cubes.

❷ Put the flour, cornstarch, and salt in the bowl of a food processor fitted with the metal blade. Using the pulse button, process 5–7 seconds to blend. Sprinkle over the frozen butter and process 3–4 times; the butter will still be in lumps.

❸ Remove the cover and evenly pour in ½ cup/4 oz of the cream, water, or a mixture of the two.

Process 5 seconds; the mixture should look lumpy, and stick together when pinched between your thumb and index finger. If the dough is dry or crumbly, add a little more liquid, and pulse just enough to blend.

❹ Turn onto a piece of plastic wrap and form into a ball. Flatten to a disk shape and wrap. Chill 20 minutes.

❺ Lightly flour a work surface and roll out the dough to a long rectangle at least 3 times longer than it is wide (about 6 x 18 inches). Brush off any excess flour.

❻ Fold the bottom third of the rectangle up and the top third down over the bottom third, as if folding a letter. Brush off any excess flour.

❼ Press edge down with the rolling pin to seal. Rotate the dough a quarter turn with one open seam face toward you and the other away from you. Roll out to the same long rectangle and fold into thirds again.

❽ Press the edges together with the rolling pin. Press your 1st and 2nd fingers into the top to make two indentations to indicate 2 "turns." Wrap dough tightly and refrigerate 30 minutes.

❾ Remove from the refrigerator; roll and fold the dough two more times, making four indentations to indicate four turns. Wrap tightly for another ½ hour before using, or chill up to 3 days.

> For light pastry, dip a solid 1-cup measure into a container of flour and, using a broad-bladed knife, level off the excess. Add ⅛ teaspoon baking powder to each 1 cup flour to ensure a lighter result.

SHAPING PUFF PASTRY DOUGH

Puff pastry should be rolled very thin, less than ⅛ inch thick, so that it can puff up easily. Once the pastry is cut out, turn it over and place on a baking sheet so the edge cut by the knife is facing up and will rise. Sprinkle a little water on the baking sheet; the steam helps the pastry rise. Many puff pastry shapes are cut out or free-form and the edges are generally scalloped, so they rise and prevent the surface from splitting. After glazing, the pastry is baked in a very hot oven to accelerate rising. The heat can then be reduced to cook the pastry thoroughly. Alternatively, slide another cold baking sheet under the hot one halfway through the cooking time, or cover the top with foil.

CHOUX PASTRY (CREAM-PUFF PASTRY)

Pâte à choux, "cabbage pastry," is so-called because the little cream puffs characteristically made from it resemble tiny cabbages. It is also used to make eclairs and profiteroles, and can be deep-fried for fritters, formed into a large cheese-flavored ring called *gougère*, or poached for little dumplings.

Making cream-puff or choux pastry is very simple. The water, butter, sugar, and salt are combined in a saucepan and brought to a boil. The flour is beaten in off the heat, then dried out slightly and the eggs added until a soft paste forms. The dough can be spooned or piped onto baking sheets while still warm, then baked until crisp and dry. The dough rises quickly and creates a lot of steam; if using an electric oven, prop the door open slightly to allow the steam to escape.

CREAM-PUFF PASTRY

INGREDIENTS
1 cup/5 oz all-purpose flour, sifted
1 cup/8 oz water
1 teaspoon sugar
½ teaspoon salt
1 stick/4 oz unsalted butter, cut into small pieces
3–4 eggs

❶ Preheat the oven to 425°F. Lightly grease a large baking sheet. Put the water, sugar, salt, and butter into a medium saucepan and bring to a boil over medium heat; the butter should be completely melted just as the water comes to a boil. (This is very important; the water should not continue boiling to melt the butter, or the proportions of the ingredients could alter.)

❷ As soon as the water boils and the butter is melted, remove the pan from heat. Add the flour mixture all at once and beat vigorously with a wooden spoon; the dough will form into a ball and pull away from the sides of the pan.

❸ Return the pan to the heat and continue to beat for about 1 minute to dry out dough as much as possible without scorching it. Remove from the heat to cool slightly.

❹ Beat in three of the eggs, one at a time, beating well. At first the mixture seems to repel the egg, then it is slowly absorbed. Beat the fourth egg lightly with a fork and add it, little by little, just until the dough is smooth, shiny, and soft enough to fall from the spoon.

❺ To form into cream puffs, use 2 spoons to shape rounds. Drop onto the prepared baking sheet at least 2 inches apart.

CREAM-PUFF PASTRY CONTINUED

6 Alternatively, spoon the pastry dough into a large pastry bag fitted with a 3/4-inch plain tip. Pressing evenly, pipe into mounds or eclair shapes, or as recipe directs.

7 Brush with a little egg wash and use a dampened fork to smooth the tops. Bake 15 minutes, then reduce the temperature to 400°F. Continue to bake 15–20 minutes longer, with the door slightly open. Bake until well puffed and golden brown.

8 Remove the baking sheet to a wire rack. Carefully pierce a hole to make a slit in the sides of the puffs or eclairs to allow the steam to escape. Return to the oven for 5–10 minutes to dry out. Remove to a wire rack to cool completely.

9 To fill the cream puffs, slice each one horizontally. Remove any uncooked or soggy dough. Spoon whipped cream or pastry cream into the bottom half of each puff and cover with the top half. Dust with confectioner's sugar or top with chocolate sauce.

TRIPLE CHOCOLATE CREAM PUFFS

12 large cream puffs or 24 small

INGREDIENTS
125 g/4 oz plain flour
2 tbsp unsweetened cocoa
    powder
25 ml/8 fl oz water
1/2 tsp salt
1 tbsp sugar
115 g/4 oz unsalted butter, cut
    into pieces
4–5 eggs

CHOCOLATE WHIPPED CREAM FILLING
300 g/10 oz fine-quality plain
    chocolate, chopped
500 ml/16 fl oz whipping cream
50 ml/2 fl oz brandy or other
    liqueur

CHOCOLATE SAUCE
300 ml/10 fl oz whipping cream
60 g/2 oz unsalted butter, cut
    into pieces
225 g/8 oz plain chocolate,
    chopped
1 tbsp golden syrup
1 tsp vanilla essence

1 Preheat oven to 220°C/425°F/ Gas 7. Lightly grease 1 or 2 large baking sheets.

2 Into a small bowl, sift together the flour and cocoa. In a medium pan over a medium heat, bring the water, salt, sugar and butter to the boil. Remove from the heat and add the flour mixture all at once, stirring vigorously until well blended and smooth and the mixture pulls away from the side of the pan. Return to the heat to cook the pastry for 1 minute, beating constantly.

3 With an electric mixer (or by hand), beat in 4 of the eggs, one at a time, beating well after each addition until each egg is well blended. The mixture should be thick and shiny and just fall from a spoon. If it is too dry, beat the fifth egg lightly and add to dough a little at a time until you reach a dropping consistency.

4 Spoon mixture into a large piping bag fitted with a large star or plain nozzle. Pipe 12 mounds about 7.5 cm/3 in across (or 24 small mounds) at least 5 cm/2 in apart on to baking sheets.

5 Bake for 35–40 minutes until puffed and firm. Remove the puffs and turn off the oven. Using a serrated knife, slice off top third of puff; return opened puffs, cut-side up, on to baking sheets and return to oven for 5–10 minutes to dry out. Remove to wire rack to cool completely.

6 Prepare chocolate whipped cream. Place chocolate in small bowl. Set the bowl over a small pan of simmering water, turn off heat and stir chocolate until it melts and is smooth. Cool chocolate to room temperature. In a medium bowl with an electric mixer, beat cream to soft peaks. Quickly fold cream into melted chocolate; fold in the liqueur. Turn into a bowl, cover and chill for 30 minutes.

7 Spoon chocolate whipped cream into a large piping bag fitted with a large star or plain nozzle. Fill each puff bottom with the chocolate filling, then cover each puff with its top.

8 To serve, in a medium saucepan over a low heat, heat the cream, butter and chocolate until melted and smooth, stirring frequently. Remove from heat and cool 10–15 minutes until slightly thickened. Pour a little sauce over each of the cream puffs and serve while chocolate sauce is warm, or refrigerate until ready to serve.

PASTRY

Fruit and Nuts

The vast range of fruit available provides endless opportunities for even inexperienced cooks to make healthy and appetizing dishes and snacks. Easy to peel and prepare, fruit can make an unusual and exotic addition to your repertoire. Nuts can easily complement fruit, as well as providing extra proteins and a crunchy texture.

Fruit

Fruits offer the cook a tremendous variety of color, flavor, and texture. Most commonly eaten out of hand as a snack, fruit appears in meals throughout the day; from sliced bananas on breakfast cornflakes to apple pie for evening dessert. Used in appetizers, salads, soups, and main courses, fruit also makes the perfect partner for cheese. It forms the basis of pickles, relishes, jams, preserves and, of course, desserts. It can be raw, poached, sautéed, battered, or deep fried, boiled, baked or puréed, and used to make mousses, sauces, pies, sorbets, and ice creams.

CHOOSING AND RIPENING FRUIT

Choose fruit which is heavy for its size. It should be fragrant and fresh-smelling, yielding slightly when pressed with the fingertips near the stem end. Allow under-ripe fruit to ripen at room temperature, then refrigerate. Buy only as much as you need, as ripe fruit cannot be stored for very long. To speed up the ripening process, place under-ripe pieces in a brown paper bag with a very ripe piece.

CLEANING FRUIT

Fruits with edible skins, such as apples, pears, plums, nectarines, and grapes, should be washed before eating. However, delicate berries should be washed *only if necessary*. Some fruits, like apples and lemons, are waxed; they should be scrubbed with soapy water before grating, julienning, or eating unpeeled.

PREVENTING DISCOLORATION

Fruits such as apples, pears, peaches, bananas, and avocados quickly turn brown when sliced. This reaction of enzymes to the air can be slowed down by rubbing the cut surfaces with an acid such as lemon, lime, orange, or grapefruit juice. Immersing the fruit in *acidulated* water is a short-term solution, but do not allow them to soak or the fruit will become waterlogged. Always prepare fruit just before it is needed.

FRUIT TYPES

Fruits can be roughly divided into eight categories: pomes, citrus, berries, grapes, drupes or stone fruits, melons, exotic, and tropical fruits. Pomes are thin-skinned tree fruits, with firm flesh and a central core containing seeds. Apples, pears, crabapples, and quinces are pomes. Tomatoes, eggplants, and peppers, are technically fruits, but are generally treated as vegetables.

PEELING AND CORING

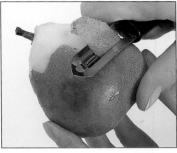

1 To peel, use a swivel-bladed vegetable peeler or small, sharp knife. Remove the peel of an apple or pear in a long spiral strip.

2 Alternatively, peel a ring from the top and bottom, then peel lengthwise, removing the skin in vertical strips. This latter method is particularly pretty when a pear is to be poached.

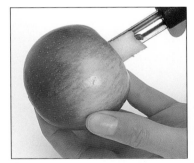

3 To remove the core, use an apple corer. Push it into the stem end of fruit, pushing out the whole core. Alternatively, use a melon baller or small spoon; scoop out the core and seeds, starting from the base and leaving stem end intact.

4 To core fruit halves, use a small knife or melon baller. Scoop out the center, then remove the stem end and bottom. For quarters, use a small, sharp knife to cut out the core and stalk.

CITRUS: PEELING CITRUS FRUITS

Citrus fruits have a thick rind containing a bitter, white pith and a thin layer of colored skin, the zest. The segments of fruit are juicy and acidic. Grapefruits, oranges, tangerines, mandarins, clementines, kumquats, lemons, and limes are the most common varieties.

❶ To peel, use a small paring knife to make 4 or 5 lengthwise slits. Beginning at the top, pull away each section of rind. Alternatively, use your thumb to loosen the skin from the stem end, pulling off the peel with your fingers.

❷ To peel larger citrus fruits, use a sharp knife to cut a slice from the top and bottom of the fruit. Set the fruit on a board, bottom down. Using the knife, cut off the rind lengthwise in thick strips, following the curve of the fruit. For smaller fruits, cut off the peel in a spiral, as when peeling an apple.

SEGMENTING CITRUS FRUITS

Grapefruit and orange segments are often used in fruit salads and as an accompaniment or garnish for other recipes.

Peel the fruit (see left). Holding the peeled fruit over a bowl to collect the juices, slide the blade of a sharp knife along one side of each membrane, then along the opposite side of the segment to free it from both sides of the membrane. Drop it into the bowl and continue with the next segment. Alternatively, cut the peeled fruits crosswise into rounds.

THE ZEST

The zest of citrus fruits contains very pungent aromatic oils. It can be grated, removed with a tool called a zester, or peeled off and cut into thin julienne strips. Citrus zest is used in many recipes from muffins and quickbreads to beef stews and sugar syrups. The pretty julienne strips make a delicate garnish for many dishes.

❶ Working over a plate or bowl, gently rub the fruit against the fine holes of a metal grater, taking only the outer colored peel and not the bitter white pith. Use a knife or rubber spatula to scrape any remaining zest from inside the grater.

❷ Holding the fruit in one hand, use a 5-hole zester to remove very thin strips of zest. Chop finely or use as is.

❸ Use a swivel-bladed vegetable peeler to remove strips of zest. Use whole to flavor soups, stews, or syrups; alternatively, make a small pile of the peel and use a large knife to cut lengthwise into thin juliennes. Blanch, if necessary, then use as directed or as a garnish.

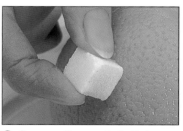

❹ Remove the scented oils by rubbing a sugar cube against the zest. Use the sugar cubes to flavor syrups and sorbets.

BERRIES: REMOVING BERRIES FROM A STEM

Berries are the small, juicy fruits of vines and bushes. They can have very thin skins like currants, or many tiny external seeds like strawberries and raspberries. Avoid buying juice-stained containers and check for any signs of mold. Refrigerate immediately and use as quickly as possible. If hand-picked or bought from a known source, avoid washing as it removes aroma and causes softening. Cultivated strawberries, wild strawberries, raspberries, red, white, and black currants, blueberries, cranberries, boysenberries, red, white, and green gooseberries, loganberries, blackberries, bilberries, elderberries, and cape gooseberries (*physalis*) are some of the many beautiful berry fruits. Currants and some smaller berries need to be removed from their stalks before using.

Using a dinner fork, slip the stalk under the prongs and pull against the berries to remove them.

GRAPES: PEELING AND SEEDING

Because of their use in wine, grapes are the largest fruit crop in the world. Grapes, vine berries that grow in large clusters, are classified as white (green) or black (red). White grapes have a thinner skin, firmer flesh, and a slightly blander flavor than black grapes. The lovely surface "bloom" is a sign of recent picking. Wash well and drain grapes before eating, using in fruit salads, or serving with cheese. Raisins and currants are all dried grapes.

If the grapes are thick-skinned, they can be peeled. Halve and seed grapes for fruit salads or leave whole and seed for use in hot dishes or sauces.

❶ Use a small, sharp knife to peel away the skin from the stalk end. If you like, cut grapes in half and use the tip of a small knife to pick out seeds.

❷ Using a sterilized tweezer or long hairpin, insert it at the stem end and twist to pull out the seeds. Alternatively, pick out with the top of a knife or vegetable peeler.

STRAWBERRIES

Remove the stem with a strawberry huller, a wide tweezer-like tool, or cut out the leaf and core with a small knife.

PIT FRUITS: PEELING

Stone fruits or *drupes* are thin-skinned fruits with soft flesh and a woody pit. Peaches, plums, apricots, nectarines, and cherries are some common varieties.

The fuzzy skin of peaches and apricots can be removed by blanching. But if cooking peaches, cook with the skin on and then remove it; the pink blush of the skin will dye the flesh underneath, giving it a beautiful glow.

❶ Score the bottom of the fruit. Lower into a saucepan of boiling water and leave for 15 to 20 seconds, depending on the ripeness of the fruit.

❷ Remove with a slotted spoon and immerse in ice water to stop cooking. Slip off the skin with your fingers or a small knife.

PITTING CHERRIES Some recipes use unpitted cherries, but always warn your guests. A cherry pitter is the best tool for tackling any quantity of fruit, especially for pies and preserves. This tool is equally efficient for pitting olives. Put the cherry in the pitter stem side up. Squeeze the handles together to push out the stone.

HALVING AND SLICING STONE FRUIT

Remove the stones from peaches, plums, nectarines and apricots before slicing for pies, grilling or stuffing and baking. Look for freestone peaches, the variety whose stone separates easily from the flesh.

❶ Taking the surface indentation as a guide, cut the fruit in half. Twist the halves in opposite directions to loosen from the stone. Pull apart.

❷ Using a teaspoon or paring knife, scoop out the stone. Rub the exposed flesh with a little lemon juice to prevent discoloration.

❸ Set cut side down on a chopping board and cut lengthways or crossways slices, as for apples.

MELONS: SLICING

Melons can be divided into 2 types: sweet or dessert melons, and watermelons. They are not suitable for cooking, being best in fruit salads, served with cured meats or made into soups and sorbets. A ripe melon should yield slightly when pressed and give off a strong perfume. Use a variety of colours for a stunning dessert effect.

❶ Cut the melon in half and use a spoon to scoop out the seeds and stringy fibres. Trim the base so each half sits flat on a plate. Serve with a slice of lemon or dash of liqueur.

❷ To serve with cured meats, cut into wedges and set each slice on a chopping board. Slide a knife between the flesh and peel to separate. Fan out slices on a plate with the meats.

❸ Alternatively, use a melon baller to scoop small balls from a melon half. Use the balls to refill the shell or use in fruit salads.

TROPICAL FRUIT GLOSSARY

Thanks to air transportation, tropical fruits are now widely available. Most are eaten raw, although some are used in cooked desserts or puréed for use in sorbets and ice creams.

Avocado This popular fruit can be eaten on its own, sliced for use in salads, mashed for dips, soups or mousses, or lightly baked.

Bananas Yellow bananas are peeled and eaten out of hand or sliced and added to fruit salad, trifle or pudding. Mashed banana adds flavour and moisture to cakes, tea breads and muffins. *Green bananas, plantains* and *cooking bananas*, are peeled and sliced, then cooked as a starchy vegetable in tropical dishes. They are not as sweet as yellow bananas and are much firmer.

Figs Best eaten out of hand, figs can be lightly baked or used in compôtes.

Kiwi fruit Bright green flesh and tiny black seeds. Kiwi also breaks down gelatine and prevents setting.

Mangoes These highly perfumed fruits can be prepared in several ways: The "hedgehog" (p.113) is often used for Thai and oriental-style meals.

Papain Natural papain, contained in papaya juice, can be used to tenderize meats but it cannot be used in gelatine-based desserts.

Passion fruit Sometimes called *grenadilla*, this dark, purple-brown wrinkled fruit has orangy-flavoured pulp and black seeds. The strong flavour is ideal for use in custards, sauces and creams.

Paw-paw (papaya) can be prepared like melon; cut lengthways, scoop out the black seeds and any fibres and serve, or cut into wedges and peel like melon wedges.

Pineapple is one of the most versatile tropical fruits. It can be cut into rings, spears and chunks, or halves of the fruit hollowed into boats and filled with its own flesh. Fresh pineapple contains an enzyme, bromelain, which breaks down gelatine, so do not use in gelatine-base desserts. Canned or cooked pineapple may be used instead.

Pomegranates The seeds of the pomegranate symbolized fertility in many ancient cultures, and its juice is still a popular Mediterranean drink.

PREPARING AND PEELING PINEAPPLE

The eyes of the pineapple should be removed with the peel. The woody core is edible, but too tough for most uses. Core before or after slicing.

❶ Use a large, heavy knife to peel for cutting into spears, rings, or chunks. Cut off the base and plume. Set the pineapple on its base on a cutting board and, working from top to bottom, cut away the peel and eyes. Unfortunately, this method does lose a lot of useful flesh.

❷ Alternatively, remove base and plume as above, and cut away the peel. Using a smaller knife, cut along one side of the eyes following the spiral and slanting the knife inward at an angle.

❸ Cut along the other side of the same spiral of eyes, slanting in the opposite direction to form a "V" shape. Lift out and remove and discard the eyes. Continue along the other rows of eyes until all are removed and whole pineapple is deeply ridged with "V" spirals. Slice into rounds or present whole.

CUTTING PINEAPPLE RINGS

❶ Set peeled pineapple on one side on a cutting board. Cut into even slices.

❷ Using a scorer or small cutter, press down around the core; lift out and discard the core.

KIWI FRUIT

❶ Remove the fuzzy brown skin with a swivel-bladed vegetable peeler or small, sharp knife.

❷ Cut crosswise into slices, cut lengthwise into wedges, or cut the unpeeled fruit in half and scoop out flesh with a spoon to eat.

PREPARING MANGOES

❶ Using the stem end as a guide to the placement of the stone, cut along each side of the stone to remove the two halves, leaving a thin section containing the stone.

❷ To create a "hedgehog," make crosswise slits, cutting through the flesh to the skin but not through it.

❸ Press on the center of the skin, as if turning it inside out, opening the cuts in the flesh. Serve as is or cut the flesh from the peel.

❹ Alternatively, cut the halves from the stone as before. Cut each half into wedges as for a melon. Slide the knife between the skin and flesh to remove the peel. Serve in wedges or dice to serve in pieces. Peel the skin from the flesh surrounding the stone and cut the flesh into pieces.

❺ Alternatively, use a swivel-bladed vegetable peeler to peel the mango. Cut off each half as above, then cut into chunks.

PREPARING AVOCADOS

Fill the cavity of an avocado half with vinaigrette, shrimp, tuna salad, or another combination, or peel and slice it to serve with salads or seafood. The Hass avocado, which is smaller with rough, black, wrinkled skin, has more flavor than the smooth-skinned, green Florida or Mexican variety.

1 Using a stainless-steel knife, cut the avocado in half lengthwise; twist halves apart like stone fruits.

2 With a chopping motion, imbed the blade of a large knife into the pit and twist to remove. Alternatively, scoop out with a rounded spoon.

PEELING AND SLICING AVOCADO

1 Run a blunt-bladed knife around the edge of an avocado half to loosen the skin from the flesh. Continue working down and around toward the rounded bottom.

2 Gently push out of the skin or peel off remaining skin, dropping the avocado, cut side down, onto a cutting board.

3 Alternatively, use a swivel-bladed vegetable peeler to peel.

4 Slice the peeled avocado half evenly crosswise or lengthwise. Use the heel of your hand to push the slices away from you, causing them to overlap, as making a pear fan. Use a metal spatula to transfer to a plate.

PREPARING POMEGRANATES

1 Using a small, sharp knife, cut out the blossom end of the fruit and score the skin in quarters.

2 Working over a bowl, break the fruit in half using the scored lines as a guide. Break the halves into quarters. (Do not cut, as the knife can puncture the kernels, releasing their juice.)

3 Scoop out the kernels with a spoon or peel back the skin, releasing the kernels. Peel off any membrane.

FIGS

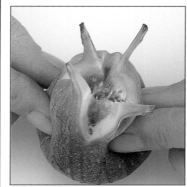

Score the fig deeply from the stem end; gently squeeze quarters apart and fill with sweetened cream cheese or nut mixtures.

COOKING FRUIT: POACHING

Although fruit is most frequently eaten in the hand or in fresh fruit salads and desserts, it forms the base of many cooked desserts. Fruits can be poached, baked, grilled and puréed, and are often used to garnish other side dishes.

Sugar and lemon are used to bring out the flavor in both uncooked fruit and in cooked fruit preparations.

Poached fruit can be served on its own, or as part of a fruit compote. Cook in a simple sugar syrup flavored with vanilla, lemon or orange zest, cinnamon, cloves, or wine, as the recipe directs.

❶ Prepare the sugar syrup; peel and core the fruit. Gently lower into the hot syrup and cover with a piece of baking parchment (this helps to keep the fruit immersed in the liquid).

❷ Gently simmer until the fruit feels tender when pierced with the point of a knife. Timing varies, depending on the fruit used and the degree of ripeness. Remove from the heat and cool in the poaching liquid.

DEEP FRYING

Some fruits can be deep-fried, but most fruit pieces are dipped in a batter before frying. The "fritters" are then sprinkled with confectioner's sugar before serving.

SAUTÉEING AND FLAMBÉEING

Lightly sautéed fruit makes an easy light dessert. Use butter to sauté, then sprinkle with sugar to caramelize. For a festive effect add a little brandy, rum, kirsch, or other liqueur and flambé, basting the fruit.

❶ In a heavy-based skillet, heat about a tablespoon of butter until it foams. Add peeled, cut-up fruit, such as apples and pears, peach slices, and raspberries, or any favorite combination. Sprinkle with a little sugar to taste and cook until lightly glazed, 1–2 minutes.

❷ To flambé, add 3–4 tablespoons of a favorite liqueur and carefully tilt the edge of the pan to allow the flame to ignite the alcohol, or hold a lighted match to the side of the pan to ignite the alcohol. Baste with the juices and alcohol until the flames die. Serve immediately.

BAKING FRUIT

Many larger fruits, like apple and quince, are baked successfully. They can be cored and used as "containers" for sweetened mixtures of nuts, raisins, or other dried fruits.

❶ To bake large fruits, core the fruit and cut a thin slice from the bottom of each to form a flat base. If you like, peel a strip from the middle of the skin to allow room for the flesh to expand without bursting.

❷ Set the fruits in an ovenproof baking dish. Baste with a mixture of butter and honey or white or brown sugar. Wine or other fruit juices can be used with other spices and flavorings. Bake in a 350°F oven until tender.

MAKING A COULIS

Coulis is a French term meaning a pourable purée and is generally applied to fruit. Usually made with puréed raw fruit, this is one of the easiest and most popular dessert sauces.

❶ Put one pound fresh raspberries, strawberries, blackberries, mango or peach slices into the bowl of a food processor. Process until smooth.

❷ Press through a strainer; add sugar and a little lemon juice to taste. A tablespoon of complementary liqueur can be added, if you like. Stir. Refrigerate until ready to serve. Thin with a little water, if necessary.

Nuts

The word nut generally refers to a seed or fruit whose edible kernel is encased in a hard shell. Nuts are an excellent source of protein and B vitamins, but are high in fat. Their high fat content makes them subject to rancidity. Keeping them in a cool, dry place, especially the refrigerator or freezer, helps slow down their deterioration.

Nuts are full of flavor, each variety quite different from the others. Largely eaten as snacks, they also add wonderful texture to many recipes, from breakfast muffins to salads and cooked dishes. Ground nuts can thicken and enrich sauces and pastries.

Because of their high fat content, they can also be pressed to produce valuable oils and spreadable pastes, such as peanut and cashew butters.

Nuts are available in many forms, from whole in their shells to ground in packages. Look for nuts that are heavy for their size with no cracks, holes, or signs of mold.

SHELLING AND SKINNING NUTS

Soft nuts like peanuts can be opened with your fingers, but most harder nuts require cracking with a nutcracker. The kernels of many nuts have a thin, papery outer skin which needs to be removed before using in recipes.

1 To skin almonds and pistachios, put the nuts in a bowl and cover with boiling water. Allow to stand 2–3 minutes, then drain. Squeeze each nut out of its skin by pinching between your thumb and index finger, or gently rub skins off while still warm.

2 To skin filberts or Brazil nuts, oven-roast (see page 117) for about 10 minutes, stirring occasionally. Wrap in a clean dishcloth and rub briskly to loosen as much skin as possible. Transfer to a fryer basket and shake off any skins which still adhere, or remove skins by hand.

CHOPPING AND GRINDING NUTS

For recipes which call for a small quantity, hand-chopping on a board, or in a curved bowl with a chopper, is the best method. For finer chopping or grinding a nut mill/grinder or food processor is best; *do not overwork* or you will end up with a paste.

1 To grind nuts: put a small amount of nuts in a nut mill or clean coffee grinder. Process a little at a time until an even texture is produced.

2 To use a food processor: process about ½ cup/2 oz nuts at a time, using the pulse button until an even texture is produced. To prevent a paste from forming, add a little flour or sugar from the recipe ingredients to avoid over-working the nuts.

3 If a nut paste is wanted, process the nuts in a food processor until a thick paste forms. Add a tablespoon of the appropriate oil and continue processing until the required texture is produced.

ROASTING OR TOASTING NUTS

Roasting or toasting nuts brings out their flavor and texture and enhances their color. Watch carefully, as their high fat content increases their tendency to burn.

❶ To oven-roast, spread nuts on a cookie sheet or shallow pan or baking sheet with edges. Bake in 350°F oven for 10–12 minutes, until golden and fragrant. Stir or shake the tray frequently. Skin or cool before using.

❷ To toast in a pan, spread nuts evenly in a dry skillet and cook over medium heat until golden. Shake pan or stir the nuts frequently to color evenly and prevent burning. Transfer to a plate or paper towel to cool.

PREPARING CHESTNUTS

Chestnuts are different from other nuts as they are particularly starchy and require cooking. They are time-consuming to skin and peel, but worth it occasionally. Whole, peeled, vacuum-packed chestnuts of excellent quality are also available.

❶ Score the bottom of each nutshell. Put in a saucepan with enough water to cover and bring to a boil.

❷ Remove from the heat, but work with the nuts while still hot. Drain a few at a time; using a small knife, pull off the hard shell and peel off the brown skin.

❸ Alternatively, pierce the shell of each nut with the point of a knife and put on a baking sheet. Broil until the shells are split, stirring occasionally. Cool slightly and peel. This method also partially cooks the nuts. Cook according to the recipe.

COCONUT: PREPARING FRESH COCONUT

This is probably the largest nut, with a hairy shell and firm flesh. The liquid, coconut water, should not be confused with coconut milk which is made by grating the flesh and soaking in milk or water before squeezing out. Unsweetened coconut milk as well as thickened and sweetened coconut cream, often used in cocktails, can be found in cans.

Choose heavy coconuts and shake them to be sure they contain lots of liquid, a sign of freshness.

Fresh coconut is used in both sweet and savory dishes.

❶ Use a small screwdriver to pierce each of the three "eyes" found at the stem end of the coconut; drain the liquid into a bowl. (Strain the coconut water afterward if using.)

❷ Put the coconut in a large heavy-duty plastic bag or wrap in an old dishtowel. Use a hammer or back of a cleaver to crack the shell open. About a third of the way down from the eyes is a "natural fault" line; if you can find this, the coconut will split in half. Break it into pieces with the hammer.

❸ Use a small, sharp knife to prize the white meat away from the shell. Store the meat in cold water in the refrigerator for 3–4 days (changing the water daily).

❹ If you like, trim or peel off the brown skin before using. Grate or shred on a box grater or in the food processor.

Bread and Cakes

Making bread is a comforting and rewarding experience. Once you understand how to capitalize on the characteristics of flour and yeast, a beautiful, well-textured loaf of bread will be part of your standard baking repertoire. Throughout the world cakes have a long-standing tradition and are often the centerpiece of many special occasions, from birthdays to weddings to christenings, as well as of many holidays.

Making Bread

The simplest breads are made of flour, water, yeast, and salt. Adding egg, sugar, milk, butter, nuts, raisins, or other ingredients will produce richer, sweeter, more cake-like breads. Using other flours, such as whole wheat or rye, cornmeal, or oats, adds texture to the dough.

The gluten content and the consistency of flour varies from region to region, season to season, and even batch to batch. Therefore, the amount of liquid any flour absorbs will vary. Gluten, a form of protein, absorbs liquid and produces elastic strands in the dough.

Yeast is the rising agent used in most breadmaking (see right). Proofing the yeast – the first step in breadmaking – ensures that the yeast is active and begins the initial fermentation. Kneading, the most important step, distributes the yeast evenly throughout the dough. Kneaded dough needs to rise at least once, sometimes twice, depending on the dough and the type of yeast.

Salt slows down the yeast's fermentation. It helps to control the rising of the dough, as well as accenting flavor. Generally, a scant tablespoon for each 450 g (1 lb) flour is about right.

Liquid binds the dough and begins the fermentation of the yeast. Water is most commonly used, but milk gives a softer texture.

USING YEAST

Yeast is very sensitive to temperature, thriving at about 85°F. At lower temperatures, it works more slowly or becomes dormant; at temperatures above 138°F it dies. It is available in two forms: compressed – also called fresh or cake yeast – and active dry yeast. Compressed yeast is more perishable and can be difficult to find. It should be a creamy beige color and have a sweet, fresh, yeasty smell. If it has a dark appearance or spots or a sour smell, discard it. Compressed yeast can be refrigerated, well-wrapped, up to 2 weeks. It is available in ½-ounce cubes and 1-pound blocks, and can be frozen up to a month. Active dry yeast is easily available and can be stored for months in a cool, dry place, although it is best stored in the refrigerator.

To dissolve or "proof" active dry yeast, whisk the yeast into warm water, allowing 3 to 4 tablespoons of water per envelope (1 scant tablespoon) of yeast. Adding a little sugar after the yeast is moistened will hasten the action. Dry yeast does not dissolve well in milk, so it should be dissolved first in warm water, then the milk added. The yeast mixture should begin to bubble and froth in 10–15 minutes. If not, discard it and start again. One envelope of active dry yeast (about 1 scant tablespoon) is equal to ½ ounce compressed or fresh yeast. Fast-acting rapid (quick)-rise or easy-blend yeast can raise bread dough in half the normal time, and it can be mixed directly with the dry ingredients.

EASY WHITE BREAD

INGREDIENTS
1 envelope (1 scant tablespoon) active dry yeast
4 tablespoons warm water (110°–115°F)
1–2 tablespoons sugar
1 cup/8 fl oz warm milk (110°–115°F)
3 tablespoons butter, diced
3¾ cups/1 pound all-purpose flour, plus extra
1 tablespoon salt
1 egg, beaten with 1 tablespoon water for glaze

❶ Put yeast in a small bowl, stir in the warm water, add a little of the sugar, and stir to dissolve.

❷ Set aside until yeast is "proofed," when fermentation causes puffing and frothing around the edge of the liquid. If it does not proof at all, discard it and start again.

❸ Meanwhile, heat milk to about 110°F and stir in butter until it is completely melted. Set aside until it is the same temperature as the yeast mixture.

❹ Sift flour, salt, and remaining sugar into a large bowl, stirring to combine. Using a large spoon, make a well in the center. Add "proofed" yeast mixture.

5 Pour the milk and butter mixture into the bowl.

6 Using a wooden spoon, gradually draw flour from the edge of the well into the liquid.

7 Continue until a soft dough forms and pulls away from the side of the bowl. If dough is too wet and sticky, sprinkle over a little more flour, a tablespoon at a time. If it is too dry, add a little more warm water.

8 Turn dough onto a lightly floured work surface. Using a stiff metal spatula, begin to knead it. Fold dough onto itself, pulling toward you, then push it away from you with the heel of your hand.

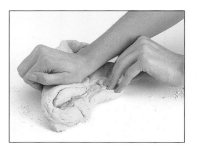

9 Rotate dough a quarter turn, repeating the action. Continue for about 10 minutes, adding a little flour from time to time, if necessary, until dough is smooth and elastic, and air bubbles form on the surface.

10 Shape dough into a ball, transfer to a large oiled bowl, and cover. Or slide it into a large plastic freezer bag, oiled inside, and seal. Set bowl in a warm, draft-free place, about 75°–80°F, for 1 to 1½ hours, until double in bulk.

11 To test if dough has risen sufficiently, push 2 fingers about 1 inch into it. If dough does not spring back, it is ready.

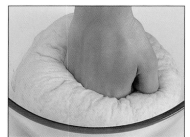

12 Punch or knock back dough by pushing a fist into the center to deflate it. Turn onto a lightly floured surface, knead lightly 1–2 minutes, and shape into a ball. Let it rest about 5 minutes. Meanwhile, lightly butter or oil two 8 x 4 x 2-inch loaf pans.

13 Using a sharp knife, cut dough in half. Form into two 8-inch ovals, gently stretching and rounding the edges. Tuck long ends under and drop each oval into a pan. Cover pans with a clean, dry dish towel or slide into a large plastic bag and seal.

14 Set in a warm place to rise again, 45 minutes to 1 hour, or until double in bulk. Preheat the oven to 450°F.

15 Brush tops with egg glaze and bake in the center of the oven 15 minutes. Reduce to 375°F and bake 20 to 25 minutes longer, until tops are well browned.

16 To test for doneness, turn a loaf out and tap the bottom with your knuckles: it should sound hollow. For a crisper loaf, remove loaves from their pans and bake on the rack 5 to 10 minutes longer. Alternatively, test with an instant read thermometer; the temperature should be about 200°F. Cool on a wire rack.

BUSY COOKS

ELECTRIC MIXER Bread may be made in a heavy-duty electric mixer fitted with a dough hook; this makes kneading easy work. Dissolve yeast directly in the mixing bowl as directed. Add remaining liquid ingredients and mix until blended. Add most of the flour and mix at low speed until blended. Increase speed to medium and knead 3–4 minutes, adding flour as needed, to produce a smooth, shiny dough.

FOOD PROCESSOR A heavy-duty food processor, fitted with the metal blade, also makes short work of breadmaking. Dissolve yeast as directed. Put dry ingredients in food processor and process 10 seconds to blend. With the machine running, pour yeast and other liquid ingredients through feed tube until the dough comes together. Let dough rest for 4–5 minutes, then process for about 45 seconds. Turn the dough onto a lightly floured surface and knead 2–3 minutes by hand to produce a smooth, shiny dough.

MICROWAVE Although the dough rises or "proves" best in a warm, draft-free place at about 80°F, a microwave can reduce the rising time by half; but be careful not to overheat the dough. Place kneaded dough in a microwave-safe bowl and cover tightly with plastic wrap. Microwave on High (100% power) for 40 seconds, let stand 10 minutes, then repeat. The dough should feel just warm. Allow to continue rising in normal conditions until double in bulk. (These times are for dough made with 1 pound of flour or more. For smaller amounts, decrease the heating time by half.)

SHAPING OTHER LOAVES

Other free-form shapes are easy to create with most classic bread doughs. Be sure to grease baking sheets or other pans.

FREEFORM ROUND
❶ For one large loaf: shape kneaded dough into a ball, gently pulling side under center to form a tighter ball.

❷ Place the ball on a prepared baking sheet seam side down. Using a sharp knife, slash top with an "X"; this is a traditional Coburg loaf.

BRAIDED LOAF
❶ Cut dough into three equal pieces. Roll each piece to a long rope shape, tapering the ends. Lie rope shapes next to each other. Beginning in the center and working toward one end, braid ropes together.

❷ Pinch ends together and tuck them under the braid. Turn dough and continue braiding the other end, pinching ends and tucking under. Transfer to a baking sheet, keeping ends tucked under.

To reduce the rising time or allow the dough to rise more slowly, refrigerate the dough, tightly covered, overnight. This slows the rising time dramatically. This technique is often used with richer doughs such as brioche, as it encourages a closer, finer-textured dough.

SHAPING ROLLS

On a lightly floured surface, shape the dough into a long, thick rope shape. Cut crosswise into equal pieces.

ROUND ROLLS
Using the palm of your hand, roll each piece against the surface to form a smooth ball. For oval rolls: roll each piece into a tapering cylinder shape. Arrange on a baking sheet 2 inches apart to allow for rising.

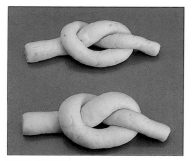

BOW KNOTS
Roll each piece into a long thin rope shape. Gently tie into a loose knot. Arrange on a baking sheet and tuck ends under.

CLOVER KNOTS
Divide each piece of cut-off dough into three pieces and roll each into a small ball. Press three balls into the cup of a greased muffin pan. Continue with the remaining pieces of dough.

MAKING PIZZA DOUGH

Pizza dough generally has a higher proportion of yeast to flour and so rises more quickly. This dough makes a large round pizza or can be baked in a 15½ x 10½-inch jelly-roll pan.

INGREDIENTS
1 envelope (1 scant tablespoon) active dry yeast
1 cup/8 fl oz warm water (110°F)
2½ cups (10 oz) strong or all-purpose flour
1½ teaspoons salt
3 tablespoons olive oil

❶ Pour about 4 tablespoons warm water into a small bowl, sprinkle over yeast, and stir with a fork to dissolve. Allow to stand 10–15 minutes to "proof," stirring occasionally.

❷ Sift flour and salt together into a large bowl. Make a well in the center. Pour in the "proofed" yeast, olive oil, and remaining water.

❸ Using a wooden spoon or your fingers, gradually draw in flour from the edge of the well, stirring until a soft dough forms and all the flour is incorporated. Allow the dough to rest about 2 minutes.

BUSY COOKS

❶ FOOD PROCESSOR Pizza dough can be made quickly in a food processor. Proof the yeast as directed. Put the flour and salt in the processor and process for 10 seconds to blend.

❷ Add the proofed yeast, olive oil, and remaining water and process until the dough begins to form a ball. Rest the dough 2 minutes, then process for about 1 minute (be careful the machine does not overheat). Turn the dough onto a lightly floured surface and finish kneading by hand for 2–3 minutes.

❹ Turn the dough onto a lightly floured surface. Knead about 5 minutes, until dough is smooth and elastic. Shape into a ball and put into a large oiled bowl. Cover tightly and put in a warm (80°F) place to rise for about 1 hour.

❺ Gently punch down dough and turn onto a lightly floured surface. Knead lightly for about 1 minute.

❻ Roll out dough to a large circle about ¼-inch thick or a rectangular shape to fit the pan. Transfer to an oiled baking sheet or the oiled jelly-roll pan. Cover with desired topping to within ¾-inch of the edge. Allow to rise about 10 minutes, then bake as directed. The edge of the pizza crust should be puffed and browned.

Quick Breads (Tea Breads) and Muffins

Quick to make and bake, quick breads are raised without yeast, using baking powder, soda, or sometimes a combination of the two. They have a soft, crumbly, cake-like texture. The chemical raising agents used react quickly with moisture and heat, causing the doughs to rise. The most popular quick breads are loaf-style versions such as banana bread, zucchini bread, and nut breads. Bran and blueberry muffins are also favorites. Other types of quick breads include biscuits, scones, coffeecakes, cornbreads, and batters used to produce pancakes, waffles, and popovers.

BAKING SODA, BAKING POWDER, AND CREAM OF TARTAR

Mixing an acid and alkali to raise dough began during the Industrial Revolution. Commercial leaveners were first marketed in the 1850s.

Baking soda combines with other acid ingredients such as buttermilk, sour cream, lemon juice, honey, or molasses to create carbon dioxide bubbles which raise the dough. This action begins almost immediately. Once in the oven, the gas is released, and the dough doubles in volume before it cooks and sets. Baking soda can also be activated by combining it with cream of tartar (an acid in powder form), then adding a liquid.

Baking powder is a combination of baking soda and an acid salt, usually cream of tartar. (Cream of tartar, an acid salt of tartaric acid, is a byproduct of wine-making.) Most baking powder is *double-acting*; this powder begins to react as soon as liquid is added, then again when heated. For this reason, doughs must be mixed and placed in the oven immediately.

Chemical raising agents should be stored in a cool, dark, dry place. Baking powder should be replaced every three to four months.

QUICK BREADS: BANANA BREAD

INGREDIENTS
¾ cup/4 oz all-purpose flour
¾ cup/4 oz wholewheat flour
1 teaspoon baking soda
½ teaspoon ground cinnamon
½ teaspoon ground ginger
½ teaspoon salt
1 stick/4 oz butter, at room temperature
¾ cup/6 oz superfine sugar
3 ripe bananas, mashed
2 eggs, lightly beaten
5 tablespoons hot water
1 cup/3 oz pecans, chopped

❶ Preheat oven to 325°F. Grease and flour an 8½ x 4½-inch loaf pan. Sift together the flours, baking soda, cinnamon, ginger, and salt and set aside.

❷ Using an electric mixer, beat butter until softened. Gradually beat in sugar until mixture is light and fluffy. Slowly beat in bananas and then the eggs. If the mixture looks curdled, add a little flour mixture.

❸ Add flour mixture alternately with the hot water in 4–5 batches. Beat until smooth. Stir in the nuts.

❹ Pour the mixture into prepared pan, smoothing the top.

❺ Bake about 1 hour, until a cake tester inserted in the center comes out clean. Cool in the pan 10 minutes, then turn onto a wire rack to cool.

Cake-making

Perfect cake-making depends on good ingredients, the correct utensils, careful measuring, accurate temperatures, and exact timing.

Most cakes are batter mixtures of flour, fat, sugar, eggs, liquid, and flavorings. Air or gas, introduced in the form of a leavening agent, makes the mixture rise while baking. Heating the gas makes the strands of gluten in the flour stretch until the cake sets. Even rising produces the characteristic spongy texture we prize so much.

There are five basic methods of cake-making. Sometimes a combination of two is used in preparing one cake. Whatever your choice of preparation, selecting and preparing the cake pan is very important. The type of pan will affect the baking time as well as the finish of the cake. A dark metal pan will reduce the cooking time slightly and encourage a darker crust; a pan with a drop-out base will help unmold fragile or delicate cakes; a springform pan is a necessity for cheesecakes, tortes (nut-based cakes), and cakes which, for any other reason, cannot be unmolded. A heavy-based cake pan prevents long-cooking fruitcakes from scorching on the bottom. Use the size and shape of pan directed in the recipe.

GRANULATED VERSUS SUPERFINE SUGAR

Many cakes and fine baked goods call for granulated sugar. Superfine sugar can be more expensive, but dissolves more quickly and easily in fragile mixtures and in batters such as a whisked layer cake or in buttercream. To make superfine sugar from granulated sugar, put the granulated sugar in the bowl of a food processor fitted with the metal blade and process for 20 seconds.

EGGS FOR CAKES

Eggs for cakes, as well as other baked goods, should always be at room temperature. Cold eggs may cause the butter and sugar mixture to curdle. The batter can be used, but the texture of the cake will not be as good. If the egg-sugar mixture appears curdled when beaten, sprinkle in about a tablespoon of the measured flour; it will help to bind it.

PREPARING CAKE PANS

With the exception of all egg-white cakes – such as angel food cakes – almost all recipes require the pan to be greased and floured before pouring in the cake batter. This prevents the cake from sticking and imparts a golden crumb finish on the bottom and side. For even easier unmolding, line the bottom and/or side with waxed paper or baking parchment. Non-stick pans are a great help but a light coating or lining is still recommended.

❶ Use a pastry brush to coat the pan with a thin layer of softened butter, margarine, or vegetable fat. Brush an even coat on the bottom, working from the center out in a pattern of rays. Then brush up the side with vertical strokes, so the entire surface is coated.

❷ Dusting the fat with a light coating of flour prevents the fat from being absorbed into the cake. Sprinkle pan generously with flour, turning and shaking to coat evenly. Tap the pan upside down over the sink to remove any excess. Finely ground bread crumbs, sugar, or finely chopped nuts can also be used as coating.

LINING CAKE PANS

For cakes which have a tendency to stick, such as whisked cakes made by the melting method, line the base of the pan with waxed paper or baking parchment.

Precut parchment cake liners are available in 8- or 9-inch diameters. They are easy to drop into a greased pan. Strips of 4-inch wide parchment are also available. This makes the lining of the sides of pans easy work.

1 Set pan bottom on a sheet of waxed paper and draw around the base to mark the diameter. Cut out the marked circle or other shape, cutting just inside the line. Press the paper onto the base of the greased pan. Grease and flour, if directed.

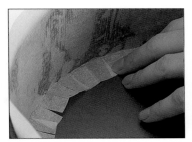

2 To line the sides of a pan for dense fruitcakes or other sticky mixtures, cut a strip of paper at least 1 inch longer than the circumference of the pan, and wide enough to extend 1 inch above the rim. Fold one long edge about ¾ inch in depth.

3 Using kitchen scissors, snip the folded edge at ½-inch intervals from the edge up to the crease. Line the sides of the greased pan with the snipped edge on the bottom, pressed into the edges of the pan. Then line the bottom. Grease and flour, if directed.

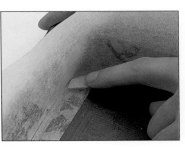

4 For a square or rectangular pan, cut and fold the measured strip of paper as for a round pan. Lay along the sides and into the corners. Snip the corners at the "L" and press the strip into the four corners, overlapping the folded edges to fit smoothly.

5 To line a muffin pan cup or bun pan, use paper liners of about the same size.

6 To line a jelly-roll pan, cut a piece of paper about 2 inches larger than the pan. Press the paper onto the bottom and into the corners of the greased pan. Snip the corners at the "L" from the top and press into the corners, overlapping the snipped edge. Grease and flour as directed.

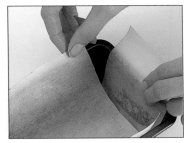

7 To line a loaf pan, use two pieces of paper. Cut one strip of paper the exact width of the pan, but 6 inches longer than the length, and fit into the pan. Cut a second strip, exactly the length, but 6 inches wider than the width. Lay this paper across the first and press into the pan. Grease the papers.

PREHEATING AND TESTING

Remember to heat your oven at least 15 minutes before baking and use an oven thermometer to verify the temperature. Most cakes are baked on the center or on the bottom third shelf. If baking two layers at once, stagger the pans so they are not directly above each other. Then rotate them from front to back, and from top to bottom, when the batter is set enough to move them.

To test for doneness, press a fingertip lightly onto the center of the cake. It should spring back if done. Alternatively, insert a cake tester or wooden toothpick into the center. It should come out clean with no crumbs attached. Most cakes shrink slightly from the side of the pan when done.

UNMOLDING AND STORING

❶ Cool cake about 10 minutes on a wire rack in its pan. Run a sharp knife around the edge to loosen any bits which may have stuck, then turn onto rack to cool completely.

❷ To avoid wire marks on the cake surface, turn onto a piece of paper, then invert it onto rack to cool completely. Store cooled cakes well wrapped or in an airtight container. Most cakes freeze well, depending on filling or frosting.

SLICING A CAKE INTO LAYERS

❶ Set the cake on a cutting board. Make 3 or 4 vertical cuts around the side of the cake. Using a serrated knife, cut the cake horizontally into layers. The vertical cuts will help realign the layers when assembling.

❷ Alternatively, pierce the whole cake around the middle with wooden cocktail sticks. Place the serrated blade above the cocktail sticks and slice, using the sticks as a guide to ensure even layers.

CREAMING METHOD: LEMON POUND CAKE

In this method the fat – usually butter or margarine – and sugar are creamed or beaten together to form a light, almost mousse-like consistency. Be sure to soften the butter to room temperature and use eggs and liquid at room temperature. Although a raising agent is usually added to ensure rising, it is the beating of the eggs which incorporates air and makes a light yet rich moist cake. Pound cakes, classic layer cakes, and many fruitcakes use this method.

INGREDIENTS
1²/₃ cups/8 oz all-purpose flour
2 teaspoons baking powder
¹/₄ teaspoon salt
2 sticks/8 oz unsalted butter, softened
³/₄ cup/6 oz superfine sugar
4 eggs, lightly beaten
1 teaspoon lemon extract
¹/₂ teaspoon vanilla extract
1 tablespoon grated lemon zest (optional)

❶ Prepare an 8 x 4 x 2-inch loaf pan as directed. Preheat oven to 325°F. Sift together flour, baking powder, and salt; set aside.

❷ Beat butter until soft in a large bowl with a wooden spoon or an electric mixer at medium speed. Gradually add sugar and continue beating at high speed until mixture is very light, moussy, and pale in color. Scrape down the side of the bowl occasionally.

❸ Add beaten eggs, a little at a time, beating well after each addition and scraping down the side of the bowl occasionally. If mixture begins to curdle, sprinkle over a little of the measured flour to help bind the mixture.

❹ Add the dry ingredients in three batches, folding in lightly by hand until just blended. (The mixer can be used, but be careful not to overbeat.) Any liquid required can be added at this point. Stir in gently, alternating with dry ingredients.

LEMON POUND CAKE CONTINUED

5 Spoon or lightly scrape the mixture into the prepared pan. Smooth the top and make a slight indentation in the center. (This helps the cake to rise more evenly, as the center usually puffs up more than the edges).

6 Bake for 50–60 minutes, until center springs back when touched. Cool 10 minutes before unmolding.

7 Dust with confectioner's sugar before serving.

SUGAR GLAZE

This simple icing is ideal for gingerbread, fruitcake, and other rich, moist cakes. Substitute lemon juice or water to suit cakes with other flavor bases.

INGREDIENTS
³/₄ cup/4 oz confectioner's sugar
1–2 tablespoons freshly squeezed orange juice

1 Sift confectioner's sugar into a small bowl and add a tablespoon of the juice. Stir until icing is smooth. Add a little more juice until pouring consistency is obtained.

2 Pour over the unmolded cake and allow to set before slicing.

ALL-IN-ONE METHOD: SIMPLE SPONGE

This method is a variation of the creamed method, but all the ingredients are mixed and beaten in one step. The classic Victoria layer cake can be made by this method.

INGREDIENTS
1¹/₄ cups/6 oz self-rising flour
1 teaspoon baking powder
¹/₄ teaspoon salt
³/₄ cup/6 oz superfine sugar
1¹/₂ sticks/6 oz unsalted butter, softened
3 eggs
1 teaspoon vanilla extract

1 Prepare two 7-in cake pans. Preheat oven to 350°F. Sift flour, baking powder, and salt into a large bowl.

2 Add sugar, butter, eggs, and vanilla extract. Beat with an electric mixer until smooth and well blended.

3 Pour into prepared pans and bake about 20 minutes. Cool and unmold as directed. Sandwich with freshly whipped cream and strawberry jam. Dust the top with confectioner's sugar before serving.

MELTING METHOD: DARK GINGERBREAD

Cakes made by this method are usually rich in sugar or syrups and have a dense moist texture. The fat is melted with the sugar, syrup, and any other liquids, and cooled before the dry ingredients and eggs are stirred in. Baking soda is usually the raising agent. Fruitcakes, gingerbreads, and some chiffon cakes are made by this method.

INGREDIENTS

1²/₃ cups/8 oz all-purpose flour
¹/₄ teaspoon salt
1 teaspoon baking soda
1 tablespoon ground ginger
1 stick/4 oz butter
¹/₂ cup/4 fl oz corn syrup
¹/₂ cup/4 fl oz molasses
¹/₂ cup/4 oz preserved ginger, finely chopped
¹/₄ cup/2 oz dark brown sugar
2 eggs, lightly beaten
³/₄ cup/6 fl oz milk

❶ Line an 8-inch cake pan. Preheat oven to 325°F. Sift flour, salt, soda, and ginger into a bowl.

❷ Assemble the butter, corn syrup, molasses, brown sugar, and preserved ginger.

❸ Combine them over medium-low heat until melted, stirring occasionally. Remove from heat and cool. Beat eggs and milk into the cooled mixture.

❹ Make a well in the center of the flour mixture and pour in the liquid mixture, stirring until smooth and well blended.

❺ Bake about 1 hour, until a cake tester or skewer inserted in the center comes out clean. Cool 10 minutes in the pan before unmolding.

RUBBED-IN METHOD: MARMALADE LOAF

This is an old-fashioned method which produces a substantial cake with a moist texture, similar to a quick bread. The fat is rubbed into the flour as in pastry making, and the raising agent is baking soda.

INGREDIENTS

1²/₃ cups/8 oz self-rising flour
¹/₂ teaspoon salt
1 stick/4 oz cold butter, diced
¹/₄ cup/2 oz superfine sugar
2 eggs, lightly beaten
3 tablespoons orange marmalade
3 tablespoons milk

❶ Prepare and line the bottom of an 8 x 4 x 2-inch loaf pan. Preheat oven to 350°F. Sift flour and salt into a large bowl.

❷ Add diced butter to flour and toss to coat with flour. Using a pastry blender or your fingertips, rub in butter until the mixture resembles medium-fine bread crumbs.

❸ Stir in sugar, eggs, marmalade, and milk until the mixture is well blended. Turn into the pan and bake about 50 minutes until a skewer comes out clean. Cool 10 minutes before unmolding.

WHISKED METHOD

This method of cake-making contains no raising agents; the light airy texture relies on the air beaten into the eggs. As the air expands in the heated oven, the cake rises. The most famous example of this cake is the French Genoise. Originally made with no fat at all, this whisked layer cake generally has a little melted butter folded into the batter at the end to enrich the cake and provide extra moisture. It is the basis for many famous cakes, jelly rolls, and desserts, but because it tends to be slightly dry, it is usually brushed with a flavored sugar syrup or liqueur and is best eaten on the day made. It also makes the perfect vehicle for a rich buttercream frosting.

This cake can be made by whisking whole eggs or by separating the eggs and whisking the yolks with the sugar as a base, then folding in the separately beaten whites with the flour at the end. This is called a "biscuit" mixture and has a slightly drier and firmer texture.

TO THE "RIBBON" STAGE

Whichever of the methods is used, the whole eggs or yolks and sugar are whisked, sometimes over heat to increase volume. When the whisk is lifted out of the bowl, the mixture should fall, leaving a "ribbon-like" trail on the surface of the mixture. If made with yolks only, the egg mixture will be thicker and more dense.

Beat eggs or yolks by hand with sugar in a stainless steel or other heatproof bowl, using a large balloon whisk. Set the bowl over, but not touching, a saucepan of *just* simmering (*not* boiling) water. Beat with an electric whisk at medium speed until the mixture is very pale and thick, forming a ribbon-trail when held over the bowl. This will take about 10 minutes. Remove from the heat and continue beating until cool.

ADDING THE BUTTER

Some recipes for whisked cakes do contain butter. If not added carefully, it can deflate the mixture, resulting in a heavy cake. Some cooks prefer the batter to be pourable, but still creamy, in which case the butter is melted. In that case, it should be completely cooled before being folded into the batter with the last portion of flour.

❶ Before the last portion of flour is added, stir some batter into the melted butter to lighten it. Carefully fold the butter mixture into the batter.

❷ Alternatively, cream butter until it is almost liquid, about the consistency of cream, but not clear or melted. Dribble it around the edge of the bowl and gently fold into batter. (Dumping it onto the surface will result in deflated batter.)

CLASSIC SPONGE CAKE

INGREDIENTS
$^3/_4$ cup/4 oz all-purpose flour
$^1/_4$ teaspoon salt
4 eggs
$^1/_2$ cup/4 oz superfine sugar
$^1/_2$ teaspoon vanilla or lemon extract
$^1/_2$ stick/2 oz softened or melted butter, optional

❶ Prepare and line the bottom of a 9-inch cake pan. Sift flour with salt, then sift again. (This is best done over a large sheet of waxed paper or a large bowl.)

❷ Whisk eggs and sugar to the ribbon stage (see left). Add vanilla extract; beat until cool. Sift flour over the mixture in 2 or 3 batches and fold in as gently as possible.

❸ If using butter, drizzle around the edge of the bowl and fold in with the last batch of flour. Pour into pan and bake about 25 minutes, until center springs back when touched lightly with a fingertip. Cool for 10 minutes before unmolding.

CLASSIC BUTTERCREAM

This is the classic frosting used to fill and frost a layer cake. The boiling sugar syrup actually cooks the egg yolks, but if you prefer, use the simple buttercream (below), which does not contain eggs.

INGREDIENTS
¼ cup/2 oz sugar
4 tablespoons water
2 egg yolks
1 teaspoon vanilla extract or grated zest of ½ lemon
1 stick/4 oz unsalted butter, softened

❶ Put sugar and water in a saucepan over low heat. Stir until the sugar is dissolved. Increase heat to high and boil until the syrup reaches thread stage (215°F).

❷ Meanwhile, put egg yolks and vanilla extract or lemon zest into the bowl of a heavy-duty mixer and begin to beat at low speed. Increase the speed and beat 2 to 3 minutes, until thickened.

❸ When the sugar syrup is ready, remove from heat. Reduce mixer speed to low and slowly pour syrup in a thin stream over egg yolks until yolks have absorbed all the syrup. Increase speed and keep beating until mixture is thick and cool, 4 to 5 minutes.

❹ Slowly beat in butter, adding it in small knobs and beating well after each addition, scraping down the side of the bowl occasionally. Allow to chill. Use to fill and frost the layer cake.

BUSY COOKS

SIMPLE BUTTERCREAM
Put *4 oz soft, unsalted butter* in a bowl and beat until soft and creamy. Slowly add *1⅔ cup/8 oz confectioner's sugar* until the mixture is pale and soft. Add one teaspoon *vanilla extract* and a tablespoon of *milk* until the frosting is spreadable. Add more milk if too thick, more sugar if too thin.

MAKING A JELLY ROLL: CHOCOLATE AND VANILLA JELLY ROLL

Jelly rolls are usually made using a sponge cake base, since the texture is just right for rolling. Use a filling of a contrasting color to accentuate the spiral effect. Dust light-colored cakes with confectioner's sugar, chocolate cakes with cocoa. The sponge cake can be made by whisking whole eggs or separating them and folding in the beaten whites later.

❶ Grease and line a 15 x 10-inch jelly-roll pan. Preheat the oven to 375°F. Prepare a classic sponge cake, but sift the flour mixture with 3 tablespoons cocoa powder.

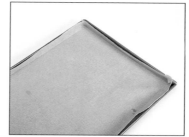

❷ Spread the mixture onto the prepared pan and spread evenly into corners. Bake 10–12 minutes, or until top springs back when touched lightly. Do not overbake.

❸ Spread a dish towel on the surface and cover with a large sheet of waxed paper, dusted with cocoa or sugar. Unmold the cake directly onto the paper-lined towel.

CHOCOLATE AND VANILLA JELLY ROLL CONTINUED

4 Peel the lining paper from the bottom of the cake and trim any crisp ends evenly from the cake.

5 Starting from one short end, gently roll the cake with the paper inside; do not wrap the towel inside the cake. Set on a rack, seam-side down, and allow to cool completely.

6 To fill, unroll the cake and spread with vanilla buttercream, ice cream, or whipped cream to within 1 inch of the edges.

7 Reroll the cake and filling. Use the paper as a guide, but do not roll the paper inside the cake.

8 Place on a serving plate or board seam-side down, and frost or sprinkle with confectioner's sugar as the recipe directs.

CHEESECAKE: CLASSIC NEW YORK-STYLE CHEESECAKE

Not technically a cake, this is a popular confection made with curd, cream cheese, or ricotta cheese. Usually baked in a springform pan lined with a crumb crust, or sometimes a pastry case, it does not have the texture of a cake, but is soft and moist. Eggs added to a creamed batter of cheese, sugar, and flavorings set the mixture, rather than making it rise. Some cheesecakes are set with gelatin and chilled unbaked.

INGREDIENTS
9-in springform pan, lined with a baked crust
2²/₃ cups/1 lb cream cheese
1¹/₄ cups/10 oz sugar
2 cups/16 oz sour cream
3 eggs
3 teaspoons vanilla extract

1 Beat cream cheese with an electric mixer, on low speed, until soft and creamy. Gradually beat in half the sugar until smooth and well blended. Beat in half a cup of the sour cream, and the eggs one at a time. Scrape down the side of the bowl occasionally. Beat in 2 teaspoons of the vanilla extract.

2 Bake in a preheated oven 325°F for about 45 minutes. Reduce heat if the cake colors too quickly. Cool 5 minutes. Beat remaining sour cream with remaining sugar and vanilla. Pour over cheesecake and bake 5–7 minutes longer. Cool on a wire rack. Refrigerate overnight.

PERFECT CHEESECAKE
The most common cause of cracks is baking at too high a temperature; in this case the outside edge sets before the center expands and settles. Baking in a water bath (wrap the pan in foil to prevent leaking) or setting a pan of water on the floor of the oven should help.

Overbeating can be another cause, or removing the cake from a hot oven to a cold surface. To combat this, underbake by 5 minutes, turn the oven off, open the door a crack, and let the cheesecake cool for an hour before removing from the oven.

Chocolate and Dessert Making

Sugar and chocolate are probably the two most important ingredients in confectionery and dessert making. Sugar is a prime ingredient of poached and candied fruits, sugar coatings, blown and pulled sugar, fondants, and caramel, and forms the base syrup for praline and nougatine. Boiled sugar sweetens fudge, toffee, taffy, caramels, and pralines. Chocolate is probably the world's favorite sweet flavoring, used as a filling as well as in truffles, fudge, and sauces. Decorations, curls, leaves and ribbons also make the most of chocolate's universal appeal.

Sugar

Sugar is the basis of candy and of sugar syrups. It is also important in preserving fruits and other foods in jams and chutneys, and gives cakes, pastries, and breads a golden color and appetizing texture. Sugar helps to "feed" yeast, preventing batter and dough from setting too quickly, and also retains moisture, adding to the keeping qualities of baked goods.

Brown sugar

SUGAR AND SYRUP GLOSSARY

We use many kinds of sugars and syrups, and our choice affects the texture, flavor, taste, and appearance of the end product. Most sugars and corn syrup will keep indefinitely, if stored in an air-tight container in a cool, dry place; maple syrup and molasses should be refrigerated after opening.

Brown sugars Brown sugars are an amalgam of granulated sugar and molasses. Dark brown sugar contains more molasses and has a stronger flavor and color. All brown sugars produce a denser, chewier texture, desirable in some cookies and cakes. These "true" brown sugars should not be confused with "brownulated" sugar, made with caramel. It should not be heated as it does not act as other sugars. Brown sugar should be firmly packed when measured by volume. Keep container tightly closed, since brown sugars tend to dry out and harden.

Coarse sugar Sometimes called decorator's sugar, it is used for decorating breads, cakes, muffins, cookies, and pastries.

Confectioner's sugar Also called powdered sugar. It should be sifted before measuring. Because it does not have a grainy texture, it is ideal in uncooked dishes, frostings, coatings and some pastry.

Golden syrup A by-product of sugar-refining, golden syrup is a light pale syrup with a subtle butterscotch flavor.

Corn syrup Corn syrup is a thick, pourable syrup manufactured from corn kernels. Because it prevents other sugars from crystallizing, it is often used in candy-making. Corn syrup also tends to absorb moisture, keeping baked goods moist. Dark corn syrup has a stronger flavor and color from added caramel.

Glucose, another thick syrup, is also derived from corn kernels.

Demerara sugar Demerara sugar, is a golden-brown, less-refined sugar with a low molasses content. Not as moist as light brown sugar, its large, sparkling crystals make it suitable for sprinkling on desserts and cereals, and decorating baked goods.

Fructose Found naturally in honey, fruit, and some vegetables, it is suitable for diabetics in small quantities. However, it is not generally suitable for all-purpose cooking.

Granulated sugar This is the most commonly used sugar. Refined from cane or sugarbeet, it has white, free-flowing, medium-sized crystals suitable for most home cooking. However, in pastry and cookies, it can show up as brown flecks. Golden granulated sugar contains a slight residue of molasses or is colored with molasses. Use as granulated sugar.

Coarse sugar

Confectioner's sugar

Golden syrup

Corn syrup

Demerara sugar

Granulated sugar

Honey Honey is probably the world's original sweetener. It can be runny or set; sometimes it is sold on the edible comb. Generally the lighter the color, the milder the flavor. Often pasteurized to prevent crystallization, it lends texture and moisture to many baked goods. Never substitute honey directly for sugar in recipes, since that will alter recipe proportions. If honey crystallizes, heat in the uncovered jar in a pan of warm water, or microwave at 100 percent power for 10–12 seconds until liquified.

Maple syrup The boiled-down sap of North American maple trees, this syrup has a rich golden color and distinctive flavor. Famous as a topping for American pancakes and waffles, 100 percent pure maple syrup is expensive, so it is often blended with other syrups; check the label.

Molasses Molasses is less sweet than other syrups, it is a characteristic ingredient of many New England dishes such as Boston baked beans, glazed hams, molasses cookies, gingerbread, and barbecue sauces. Light molasses is the residue from the first boiling of the sugar-cane juices; dark molasses comes from the second boiling. Black-strap molasses is the very dark, strong residue from the third boiling.

Molasses sugar This soft, fine-grain, dark brown sugar is one of the least refined raw sugars. Its strong taste is detectable in dark-colored baked goods such as Christmas puddings, gingerbreads, chutneys, and treacle toffee.

Muscovado sugar Soft, fine-grained brown *muscovado* sugar is made from unrefined or raw-cane sugar. The pale golden color and delicate flavor of light muscovado are appreciated in cakes and baked goods, meringues, and fudge, as is *turbinado*, whose steam-washed crystals have a delicate molasses flavor, golden caramel color, and pour easily. Dark muscovado is moister with a deeper color and strong molasses flavor. It is useful when a richer flavor is wanted.

Preserving sugar This coarse crystal sugar is produced for jam, and preserve-making. Because it does not form a mass on the bottom of the pan, it prevents scorching. It also produces less scum on the surface, thus eliminating much skimming. Some preserving sugars contain pectin, the setting agent required in jams.

Raw sugar True raw sugar is the dark, sticky residue produced by boiling down cane sugar juices. In some sugar-producing countries, this residue is poured into molds to harden for use as a sweetener.

Alternatively, the residue is separated into molasses and "raw" sugar which then can be refined into white sugar, or purified into a variety of brown sugars. In many countries, completely raw sugars are banned because of possible contamination.

Rock sugar This is a crystallized clear or golden, large-crystal sugar, sometimes lightly crushed to decorate cakes and cookies; it is also used as a coffee sweetener.

Superfine sugar A white, free-flowing sugar with very fine crystals, this is ideal for baking. Since it creams easily and dissolves easily in liquids, it is the preferred choice for pastries, cookies, custards, and drinks. Superfine sugar can be made easily in the food processor. Put a measured amount of granulated sugar in the bowl of a food processor fitted with the metal blade, and process until finely ground.

To help retain moisture, store the sugar in a plastic bag, and place the bag in a plastic box. Add a slice of apple, potato, or bread to the box.

Honey

Maple syrup

Molasses

Molasses sugar

Muscovado sugar

Preserving sugar

Rock sugar

A sugar syrup is a solution of sugar dissolved in water. If a sugar syrup is boiled, the water will begin to evaporate, changing the concentration. As the syrup is boiled beyond the saturation point, the properties of the sugar change from a boiled sugar syrup to caramel.

Simple sugar syrup is used for poaching fruit, moistening cakes, adding to fruit salads or sauces, and as the base of many sorbets. Flavorings such as vanilla, cinnamon, orange, or lemon juice can be added.

❶ To make a simple sugar syrup, heat water and granulated or superfine sugar in a saucepan over low heat, stirring occasionally until the sugar dissolves. *The sugar must be completely dissolved before boiling or crystals will be likely to form.*

❷ Bring the dissolved sugar water mixture to a boil over medium-high heat. Once the mixture boils, do not stir – this can encourage crystals to form.

❸ Boil the syrup for 1 minute until it looks crystal clear.

To measure honey and other sticky syrups, generously oil the measuring spoon. This allows the syrup to slide off more easily.

Chocolate

Chocolate comes from the cacao tree. Its scientific name *theobroma cacao*, meaning "food of the gods," indicates that even centuries ago it was known to be an extraordinary food. The cacao tree produces large pods which contain about 40 almond-sized cocoa beans. After ripening, the beans are removed from the pods to be dried in the sun and fermented, then cured and roasted to develop flavor and reduce bitterness. The beans are finally crushed to yield the cocoa *nib*. It is this nib that is processed into the chocolate that we know.

Once shipped to various chocolate producers around the world, the nibs are roasted again and crushed to produce a paste or mass called *chocolate liquor*. This mass or liquor contains about 53 percent fat – called *cocoa butter* – and cocoa solids. When the paste hardens, it is compressed and kneaded by heavy rollers in a process called "conching," named after the shell-shaped rollers. This process produces the smooth, mellow product we call chocolate. It is the blending of beans, the method and duration of roasting, the length of time conching, and the proportion of cocoa butter and solids in the end product which determine the flavor and quality of all commercial chocolates.

COOKING WITH CHOCOLATE

Chocolate is the result of an emulsification process, the homogenization of two substances. It must be treated very carefully: the two most important factors in handling chocolate are *temperature* and *moisture*.

Chocolate should never be heated above 118°F as it can burn easily, developing a bitter flavor and gritty texture. Milk chocolate and white chocolate are even more delicate, since they contain milk solids. They should not be heated above 110°F. Chocolate melted on its own must not come into contact with moisture, as even a drop of water or steam can cause the chocolate to "seize" or "block," becoming a thick dry unworkable paste. For this reason, make sure all equipment is *perfectly dry*. Never cover chocolate during melting as any steam droplets could drip into the chocolate.

Plain, bittersweet, and semisweet chocolate

Unsweetened chocolate

Couverture or covering chocolate

White chocolate

Milk chocolate

Cocoa powder

Chocolate chips

Chocolate is found in many popular guises; from solid to pre-melted, dark through white, deeply brown and bitter to milky and sweet; even powdered, as cocoa. Chocolates owe their different tastes to the quality and roasting of the beans, the style of production, and the national preferences of the country in which the chocolate was manufactured.

Brand-name chocolate is made from chocolate liquor blended with additional cocoa butter, sugar, and flavorings. The more chocolate liquor and cocoa butter the chocolate contains, the better the quality. Every country of production sets minimum standards. Although certain types of chocolate lend themselves to particular preparations, even that can be very much a personal preference.

Plain, bittersweet, and semisweet chocolate This dark chocolate varies from bittersweet to the slightly sweeter plain and semi-sweet chocolate. It contains only chocolate liquor, cocoa butter, and sometimes lecithin (an emulsifier) and sugar in varying quantities. Sometimes vanilla is added as extra flavoring. Guidelines for chocolate solids vary from country to country, which accounts for the wide variety of quality. In the U.S., dark chocolates must contain 34 percent solids. Best results in cooking are obtained with chocolate which contains a minimum of 50 percent chocolate solids. Although the three types are interchangeable, bittersweet chocolate gives a stronger flavor to most recipes.

Unsweetened chocolate Also called Baker's Chocolate or bitter chocolate (*not* bittersweet), unsweetened chocolate is the cooled chocolate liquor with a quantity of cocoa butter reblended into it. It has a bitter,

intense, full chocolate flavor and is used mainly in manufacturing chocolate products and in home-baked chocolate recipes, especially cakes and brownies. An adequate substitute for 1oz unsweetened chocolate for baking is ³⁄₄oz cocoa powder plus ¹⁄₂oz unsalted butter. The sugar in the recipe will need to be adjusted.

Couverture or covering chocolate This fine, richly flavored chocolate, with a smooth texture and shiny appearance, has a very high proportion of cocoa butter. It is expensive and mainly used by professionals for coating and dipping other chocolates and is not generally used in baking or dessert-making. This chocolate must be tempered (p.137).

Do not confuse couverture with commercial coating chocolate or cake covering. These are easier to use, but lack the flavor and gloss of couverture.

White chocolate Technically, white chocolate is not chocolate at all because it does not contain any chocolate liquor. It is becoming more popular and is used in cakes, mousses, sauces, and desserts and as a contrast with other chocolates. As with milk chocolate, it is sensitive to heat, so be careful when melting it. Use a double boiler and keep the temperature below 120°F.

Milk chocolate Milk chocolate has a lower cocoa solid content, about 15 percent, and has dried milk powder added. This, and its much milder flavor, means that it cannot be substituted for bittersweet, dark, or semisweet chocolate in baking and dessert recipes. It scorches easily when melting, so melt in a double saucepan.

Chocolate chips Originally produced for use in chocolate-chip cookies, these little pieces are available plain, milk, and white, as well as in mini-sizes. Because they were designed to keep their shape when heated, they are best used in cookies, cakes, and baked goods where they add extra texture and interest.

Cocoa powder Ground and sifted, this powder gives the most intense chocolate flavor to baked goods and desserts. Sift the cocoa powder with other dry ingredients or dilute with boiling water to form a paste, much like cornstarch, before adding to other mixtures.

Drinking chocolate is composed of cocoa powder with added sugar and sometimes dried milk solids. Do not confuse it with cocoa powder.

MELTING CHOCOLATE

There are several ways of melting chocolate, but no matter what method is used, it should be melted slowly. Chocolate can be melted on its own in a double saucepan, in the microwave, or in a very low oven. Remember, melted chocolate should feel *warm*, not hot.

Adding a liquid helps prevent chocolate from burning, but you must add enough to avoid seizing. Chocolate marries well with butter, cream, milk, water, coffee, or a liqueur, and generally 1 tablespoon of liquid for each 2 oz of chocolate is sufficient.

ON A STOVE
To melt chocolate on its own on top of the stove, put the chocolate in the top of a double boiler or in a bowl set over very hot, simmering water. The base of the pan or bowl should not touch the water. Allow the chocolate to stand several minutes to soften, then begin to stir occasionally until it begins to melt. Stir until completely melted and smooth.

TO "LOOSEN" SEIZED CHOCOLATE
Stir in about 1 teaspoon white vegetable fat or oil for each ounce of chocolate. Do not use butter or margarine as they contain water. If it does not work, start again with new chocolate. Do not discard the seized chocolate, however; it can be used in a recipe which melts chocolate in another liquid.

WITH A LIQUID OVER DIRECT HEAT
Put the chopped or broken pieces of chocolate in a heavy-based saucepan. Add the measured amount of liquid or butter. Set over low heat and stir frequently, until melted and smooth. Remove from the heat.

TEMPERING CHOCOLATE

"Tempering" is a process of slowly heating and cooking chocolate to stabilize the emulsified cocoa solids and cocoa fat. It is generally used by professionals in recipes that require *couverture* chocolate, which shrinks quickly for easy release from molds, and can be kept at room temperature for weeks without losing its crispness and shiny surface. Untempered chocolate should be refrigerated immediately to solidify the cocoa butter and prevent it from rising to the surface causing fat bloom.

All solid chocolate is tempered in production, but once melted it loses its "temper" and must be retempered.

❶ Melt the couverture chocolate by one of the methods on the left. The temperature should be about 110°F; check with an instant-read or candy thermometer. Stir to be sure the chocolate is completely melted and smooth.

❷ Pour about three-quarters of the chocolate onto a marble slab or work surface. Using a metal palette knife or rubber scraper, scrape into a pool in the center, then spread out again. Work the chocolate in this way for 3–5 minutes until no streaks remain.

❸ Scrape the chocolate back into the bowl and stir into the remaining chocolate until well blended. The temperature should now be 90°F. The chocolate is tempered ready for use.

GRATING CHOCOLATE

Chocolate can be grated by hand, in a food processor, or in a nut grater. Having the chocolate at the correct temperature will help.

To grate chocolate with a box grater, chill the chocolate. Hold it, using a folded paper towel or foil to prevent the heat of your hand from melting it. Place the grater over a plate or bowl and rub the chocolate firmly against the grater.

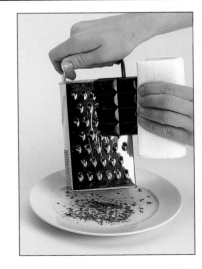

COATING WITH CHOCOLATE

Candy and small pieces of fruit can be coated in chocolate. Using tempered chocolate is ideal, but melted bittersweet or semisweet chocolate also can be used if it is refrigerated after cooking until needed.

 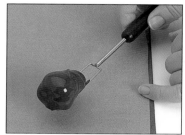

❶ Melt (or remelt) the chocolate and pour into a deep bowl. The temperature should be between 115–120°F. Use a special chocolate dipping fork, skewer, or fondue fork to lower the candy or fruit into the chocolate.

❷ Turn to coat completely, then lift out of the melted chocolate. Tap gently and scrape on the edge of the bowl to remove the excess chocolate.

❸ Set on a baking sheet lined with baking parchment. Draw the tines of the dipping fork across the top, lifting lightly, to leave two raised edges.

CHOCOLATE LEAVES

Use any fresh, non-toxic leaves with prominent veins, such as rose or lemon. Wash and dry them well before coating with chocolate. Refrigerate the chocolate leaves until ready to use.

Using a pastry brush, brush melted chocolate over the veined side of the leaf, coating evenly and completely. Set on a paper-lined baking sheet and refrigerate to set. Starting at the stem end, gently peel away the leaf.

CHOCOLATE SHAPES

These easy-to-make shapes are prepared with melted chocolate and can be refrigerated for up to 2 weeks.

❶ Pour the tempered or melted chocolate onto a sheet of baking parchment. Spread evenly to a thickness of ⅛ inch. Allow to set 30 minutes, or until just firm. Using a straightedge and a long-bladed knife, trim the edges to make a perfect rectangle.

❷ Using the straightedge, mark even squares, rectangles, or diamonds. Cut through with the knife.

❸ Alternatively, use small cookie or aspic cutters to cut out decorative shapes.

❹ Punch a hole in the top of the shapes, using a small, plain decorating nozzle. Thread with ribbons to make chocolate ornaments. If you like, pipe with chocolate in a contrasting color to decorate.

DRIZZLED CHOCOLATE

Chocolate can be piped into designs such as flowers, butterflies, or names. Lay a piece of baking parchment over the desired shape and trace over it. Alternatively pipe random shapes directly onto the paper.

❶ Spoon melted chocolate into a paper cone (see page 139) or small piping bag fitted with a very small, plain decorating nozzle. Drizzle onto the paper following the shape of the tracing. Allow to set about 30 minutes, until firm, before peeling off the paper.

❷ To make butterflies, pipe chocolate onto individual squares of baking parchment; leave until just beginning to set. Fold the parchment square gently, placing the "V" shape in the indentations of an egg carton or other holder. Chill until set.

CHOCOLATE AND DESSERT MAKING

MAKING A PAPER CONE

A paper cone is ideal for piping small amounts of messy liquids like chocolate and royal icing. Small and easy to handle, it is disposable, eliminating messy cleaning up.

❶ Fold a square of baking parchment or waxed paper in half to form a triangle. With the triangle point facing toward you, fold the left corner down into the center.

❷ Fold the right corner down and wrap completely around the folded left corner, forming a cone. Fold the ends into the top of the cone. Spoon melted chocolate or other liquid into the cone and fold the top edges over to enclose the filling.

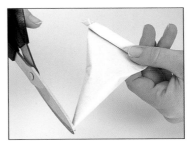

❸ When ready to pipe, snip off the end of the point, making a hole about ⅛ inch in diameter. Roll down the top of the cone to compress the filling. Use to pipe designs.

❹ Alternatively, snip off one corner of a heavy-duty freezer bag and drop in a small decorating nozzle, pushing well into the corner. Fill with melted chocolate, twisting the top to seal and to squeeze filling into the nozzle.

EASY CHOCOLATE TRUFFLES

Simple chocolate truffles are surprisingly easy to make. Roll in cocoa or chopped nuts, or coat with tempered chocolate and decorate more elaborately.

INGREDIENTS
8 oz fine-quality bittersweet or plain chocolate, chopped
6 tablespoons heavy cream
1–2 tablespoons brandy or rum
cocoa powder for rolling

❶ Melt the chocolate in a double boiler or in bowl set over hot water. Alternatively, use a microwave.

❷ Remove the melted chocolate from the heat and stir in the cream until well blended. Cool to room temperature and stir in the brandy and rum. Refrigerate until the mixture is firm enough to shape – about 30 minutes.

❸ Sift a little cocoa into a small bowl or shallow plate. Shape teaspoonfuls of the truffle mixture into balls, rolling gently between your fingers or palms.

❹ Roll the balls in the cocoa to coat completely. Use a fork or slotted spoon to remove from the coating, tapping off any excess. Set on a baking sheet and repeat with remaining mixture. Refrigerate until ready to eat.

Some Dessert-Making Techniques

Many desserts require techniques for setting mixtures, lining molds, or preparing sugar mixtures which may appear in other chapters in this book. This section includes techniques such as dissolving gelatin, lining a charlotte mold, and filling a piping bag. These techniques are useful in a number of specific recipes.

WORKING WITH GELATIN

Gelatin is available in powdered or sheet form and acts as a thickener, giving shape and body to both desserts and savory dishes. It has no flavor and is easy to use. Powdered gelatin is prepackaged in ¼ oz/1 tablespoon packets in the U.S. Sheet gelatin must be weighed, 6–7 sheets weighing about ½ oz. The amount required is determined by the other ingredients in the recipe; soft, light mixtures need less gelatin than heavy, creamy ones. In general, 1 packet of American gelatin will set 2 cups/1 pint liquid.

UNMOLDING GELATIN DESSERTS

Many gelatin-based desserts are set and then unmolded. The set dessert needs to be loosened before unmolding. If possible, use a thin tin mold, which conducts the heat and cold quickly. Before filling with the mixture, rinse the mold with cold water, allowing a few drops to stay in the bottom. This creates a small pocket of air between the mold and the mixture and helps with unmolding later.

❶ To unmold, dip the filled mold into hand-hot water just to the rim. Leave 2 seconds, or longer for ceramic or porcelain molds. Lift out and wipe dry.

❷ Slide the tip of a sharp knife between the mixture and the edge to break the air lock. Or, using your fingertips, gently pull the set mixture away from the rim.

❸ Center a serving plate over the mold and, holding them tightly together, quickly invert the mold and dish.

❹ Give a sharp downward shake. You should feel the dessert drop onto the plate. If it does not, cover the bottom of the mold with a hot, wet cloth for 10 seconds and try again. Once unmolded, wipe any drips from the plate and refrigerate immediately to reset the surface.

DISSOLVING GELATIN

Gelatin should be first softened before melting or dissolving. It should also be about the same temperature as the mixture to which it is added. If it is too cold, it will begin to set immediately, causing lumps. Once added to the mixture, it must be stirred for even distribution and to prevent it from setting on the bottom of the container. Chilling the mixture over ice while stirring is the quickest way to set the mixture. Once it begins to feel thick, remove from the ice. Fold in any whipped ingredients, then pour into the mold.

TO SOFTEN POWDERED GELATIN
Sprinkle it over a measured amount of liquid in a small bowl as the recipe directs. Allow about 3–4 tablespoons of water or juice per 1 tablespoon gelatin. Allow to soften about 5 minutes, without stirring. It will look opaque and spongy.

TO SOFTEN SHEET OR LEAF GELATIN
Put the sheets in a large bowl or baking dish. Cover with cold water and leave to soften for 5–10 minutes. Squeeze out the excess water with your hands and transfer to a small bowl for melting/dissolving.

❶ To melt or dissolve the gelatin, set the bowl of softened gelatin over a saucepan of just simmering water and heat gently until melted. Do not stir until completely melted or it may become stringy. Cool slightly. Alternatively, heat the softened gelatin in the microwave at 10–15 second intervals on 100 percent (full) power.

❷ Gradually add the melted gelatin to the prepared mixture. Set over a bowl of ice water. Stir slowly, but constantly, until the mixture begins to thicken. Fold in remaining ingredients. Refrigerate as directed.

LINING A MOLD

Many desserts use molds or pans lined with cookies or cake. The famous *charlotte russe* is lined with ladyfingers, the *charlotte royal* uses a deep bowl lined with slices of jelly roll, and the *marquise* is usually molded in a loaf pan lined with champagne cookies. Before filling, line the bottom of the mold with baking parchment; butter the paper and sides of the mold.

CHARLOTTE MOLD

❶ To line a charlotte mold with ladyfingers or champagne cookies, trim about 8 fingers into tear shapes, cutting to fit closely together in a circle. Arrange them in a daisy shape on the bottom of the mold, round side down.

❷ Trim the remaining ladyfingers to the height of the mold and place them, rounded-side out, all around the side. Fill any spaces with the trimmings to prevent filling from leaking out. Trim the tops level with the rim and pour in the mixture. Line the top with cookies to make a base.

TO LINE A BOWL

Spray a deep pyrex or other mixing bowl lightly with a vegetable cooking spray; alternatively oil lightly by hand. Cut the jelly roll into ¼-inch slices. Beginning at the base, cover the bottom and sides of the bowl with the slices pushing them tightly together. Do not overlap.

Pour the filling mixture into the lined bowl and allow to set. If the recipe directs, use any trimmings to make a base.

TO UNMOLD

Run a sharp knife between the edge of the mold or bowl, and the cookies or cake slices. Invert the dessert onto a serving plate and give a firm downward shake to unmold onto the plate. Lift off the mold or bowl.

MAKING A PAPER COLLAR

A paper or foil collar is often used on cold soufflés to support the mixture as it sets; once it is removed the dessert looks like a hot soufflé. Use baking parchment or foil, and kitchen string or tape to secure the paper.

❶ Cut a sheet of baking parchment or foil about 2 inches larger than the circumference of the dish. Fold it lengthwise in half and spray with vegetable cooking spray or lightly brush with oil.

❷ Wrap around the dish and secure with the string or tape. It should extend well above the dish rim. Fill with the soufflé mixture and refrigerate until set.

❸ To serve, remove the string or tape. Gently peel off the paper or foil, guiding it away with a knife.

FILLING A PIPING BAG

Many recipes call for decorating desserts with piped whipped cream, or shaping cookies or pastries using a pastry bag with metal or plastic nozzle or tip.

❶ To assemble the bag, drop the nozzle or tip into the bag, pushing it down to the hole at the end. Twist the bag gently while tucking it into the tip. This tightens the fit and prevents any liquid or soft filling from leaking out before you are ready to pipe.

❷ Fold over the top 2 inches of the bag to form a collar over your hand. Alternatively, put the bag, nozzle-end first, into a measuring cup or small bowl to keep it steady.

❸ Supporting the bag with one hand, gently spoon in the piping mixture with the other, scraping the spoon against the folded edge.

❹ When the bag is filled, fold the edges of the bag. Hold them together and twist the top, forcing the mixture into the tip and squeezing out excess air. Keep the top twisted closed between the thumb and palm of one hand, cupping the bag itself in your other hand. Begin to pipe.

INDEX

Quarto Publishing would like to thank the following
for supplying equipment for photography:

Kenwood Appliances plc
New Lane
Havant
Herts PO9 2NH

Prestige Group UK plc
PO Box 95
Colne Road
Burnley BB11 2AD

Pyrex
Customer Relations Department
Wearglass Works
Sunderland SR4 6EB

Tefal UK Ltd
11–49 Station Road
Langley
Slough
Berkshire SL3 8DR

Weights and Measures

WEIGHTS

Metric	Imperial
8 g	¼ oz
15 g	½ oz
20 g	¾ oz
25 g	1 oz
30 g	1 oz
45 g	1½ oz
50 g	1¾ oz
55 g	2 oz
75 g	2½ oz
85 g	3 oz
100 g	3½ oz
115 g	4 oz
125 g	4½ oz
140 g	5 oz
150 g	5½ oz
170 g	6 oz
175 g	6½ oz
200 g	7 oz
210 g	7½ oz
225 g	8 oz
250 g	8½ oz
255 g	9 oz
275 g	9½ oz
285 g	10 oz
300 g	10½ oz
325 g	11 oz
350 g	12 oz
375 g	13 oz
400 g	14 oz
425 g	15 oz
450 g	16 oz (1 lb)
550 g	1¼ lb
675 g	1½ lb
700 g	1⅔ lb
800 g	1¾ lb
900 g	2 lb
1 kg	2¼ lb
1.35 kg	3 lb
1.5 kg	3½ lb
1.8 kg	4 lb
2 kg	4½ lb
2.3 kg	5 lb
2.5 kg	5½ lb
2.7 kg	6 lb
3 kg	6½ lb
3.2 kg	7 lb
3.5 kg	8 lb
4 kg	9 lb
4.5 kg	10 lb
5 kg	11 lb

VOLUME

Metric	Imperial		American
5 ml	—	1 tsp	1 tsp
10 ml	—	2 tsp	2 tsp
20 ml	—	1 tbsp	1½ tbsp
30 ml	1 fl oz	1½ tbsp	2 tbsp
50 ml	2 fl oz	3 tbsp	¼ cup
60 ml	2½ fl oz (½ gill)	3½ tbsp	¼C + 2 tsp
75 ml	3 fl oz	4 tbsp	½C (6 tbsp)
100 ml	4 fl oz	¼ pint	½C (¼ pint)
150 ml	5 fl oz (1 gill)	¼ pint	¾C
175 ml	6 fl oz	—	¾C
200 ml	7 fl oz	—	—
250 ml	8 fl oz	⅓ pint	1C (½ pint)
300 ml	10 fl oz (2 gills)	½ pint	1¼C
350 ml	12 fl oz	—	1½C
400 ml	14 fl oz	⅔ pint	1¾C
450 ml	15 fl oz	¾ pint	—
500 ml	16 fl oz	—	2C (1 pint)
550 ml	18 fl oz	—	2¼C
575 ml	20 fl oz	1 pint	2½C
600 ml	21 fl oz	—	2¾C
700 ml	25 fl oz	1¼ pint	3C
750 ml	27 fl oz	—	3½C
800 ml	28 fl oz	—	3⅔C
850 ml	30 fl oz	1½ pints	3¾C
900 ml	32 fl oz	1⅔ pints	4C
1 litre	35 fl oz	1¾ pints	4½C
1.1 litre	40 fl oz	2 pints	5C
1.3 litre	48 fl oz	2⅔ pints	6C
1.5 litre	50 fl oz	2½ pints	6¼C
1.66 litre	56 fl oz	2¾ pints	7C
1.75 litre	60 fl oz	3 pints	7½C
1.8 litre	64 fl oz	3¼ pints	8C
2 litre	72 fl oz	3½ pints	9C
2.1 litre	76 fl oz	3⅔ pints	9½C
2.2 litre	80 fl oz	3¾ pints	10C
2.25 litre	84 fl oz	2 quarts	10½C

TEMPERATURE

°C	°F	Gas mark
3	37	
10	50	
16	60	
21	70	
24	75	
27	80	
29	85	
38	100	
41	105	
43	110	
46	115	
49	120	
54	130	
57	135	
60	140	
66	150	
71	160	
77	170	
82	180	
88	190	
93	200	
96	205	
100	212	
107	225	¼ (vc)
110	228	
115	238	
120	250	½
130	275	1
140	285	
150	300	2 (c)
160	325	3 (w)
180	350	4
190	375	5 (m)
200	400	6 (lh)
220	425	7
230	450	8 (h)
250	475	9 (vh)
260	500	

LENGTH

Metric (cm)	Imperial (in)
0.3	⅛
0.6	¼
1	½
2	¾
2.5	1
5	2
15	6
30	12 (1 ft)
46	18
92	36 (1 yd)
100 (1 m)	39